Abraham and Ibrahim
The Bible and the Qur'an Told to Children

Abraham and Ibrahim
The Bible and the Qur'an Told to Children

Francien van Overbeeke-Rippen
Study Guide by Kenneth and Margaret Thomas

Bridge Resources
Louisville, Kentucky

© 2006 Bridge Resources, Presbyterian Church (U.S.A.), Louisville, Kentucky

All rights reserved. No part of this book may be produced or transmitted in any form or by any means, electronic or mechanical, including photocopying, recording, or by any information storage or retrieval system, without permission from the publisher. For information or a complete listing of Witherspoon Press publications, contact Congregational Ministries Publishing, Presbyterian Church (U.S.A.), 100 Witherspoon Street, Louisville, KY 40202-1396. Additional copies of this book may be obtained by calling 1-800-524-2612.

Unless otherwise noted, Scripture quotations are from the New Revised Standard Version of the Bible, copyright © 1989 by the Division of Christian Education of the National Council of the Churches of Christ in the U.S.A. Used by permission.

Writer and translator: Francien van Overbeeke-Rippen
Study Guide writers: Kenneth and Margaret Thomas
Editor: Tricia Tedrow
Book interior and cover design by Jeanne Williams
Illustrations: Stewart J. Thomas

Published by Bridge Resources
Louisville, Kentucky

Web site address: www.pcusa.org/bridgeresources

Printed in the United States of America

06 07 08 09 10 11 12 13 14 15 — 10 9 8 7 6 5 4 3 2 1

Library of Congress Cataloging-in-Publication Data

Overbeeke-Rippen, Francina van
  [Ibrahiem en Abraham. English]
  Abraham and Ibrahim : the Bible and the Qur'an told to children / Francien Van Overbeeke-Rippen ; study guide by Kenneth and Margaret Thomas ; writer and translator, Francien Van Overbeeke-Rippen.
    p. cm.
  ISBN 1-57153-072-X (pbk. : alk. paper)
  1. Koran--Relation to the Bible--Juvenile literature. 2. Christianity in the Koran--Juvenile literature. 3. Islam--Relations--Christianity--Juvenile literature. 4. Christianity and other religions--Islam--Juvenile literature. I. Title.
BP134.B4O9413 2006
297.1'222--dc22
                                      2006009623

Contents

Introduction   1

Unit 1 The First Stories
The Creator and the Creation   3
Humankind   9
The First Sons   13
Nuh/Noah   17

Unit 2 Ibrahim/Abraham
Ibrahim/Abraham   23
Ibrahim and Lut/Abraham and Lot   25
The Sons of Ibrahim/Abraham   29
The Sons of Isma'il/Ishmael and Ishak/Isaac   33

Unit 3 Ya'kub/Jacob
The Sons of Ya'kub/Jacob   37
Yusef/Joseph in Egypt   39
The Sons of Ya'kub/Jacob Go to Egypt   43
Ya'kub/Jacob in Egypt   49

Unit 4 Musa/Moses
The Birth of Musa/Moses   53
Musa/Moses in the Royal Palace   57
Musa/Moses in the Land of Midian   59
Musa/Moses Called by God   61
Musa/Moses and Harun/Aaron Go to Fir'awn/Pharaoh   65
Musa/Moses with the Israelites through the Red Sea   71

Unit 5 The Desert Journey
Beginning of the Desert Journey   75
In the Desert of Sinai   79
God and Idol   81
The Commandments   87
In the Desert of Paran   91
Back into the Desert   99

Unit 6 Guides, Judges, and Kings
Guides and Judges   105
Israel's First King—Talut/Saul   109
Dawud/David—King of Israel   113
King Sulaiman/Solomon   117
Kings and Prophets   121
Exile   125

Unit 7 The Births of Jesus/'Isa and John/Yahya

Zakaria/Zachariah and His Wife, Elizabeth   129
The Child Yahya/John   133
Maryam/Mary   135
Mary/Maryam   139

Unit 8 'Isa/Jesus and Muhammad

The Child 'Isa/Jesus   143
The Child Jesus/'Isa   145
Yahya and 'Isa—John the Baptist and Jesus   149
'Isa/Jesus and His Disciples   153
Jesus/'Isa   159
Muhammad   161

Study Guide   163
Activities Instruction Section   224
Reproducible Resources   237
Glossary   249

Introduction

Have you ever heard of Ibrahim? Perhaps there is a Muslim boy in your classroom with the same name. But I don't mean him. I mean the other Ibrahim.

I mean the Ibrahim from the Qur'an, the holy book for the Muslims, written in the Arabic language. That book tells us a lot about Allah. Allah is the Arabic word for God, the Creator of heaven and earth. In the Qur'an is also written what happened many many years ago, so it tells us about Ibrahim too.

Perhaps you even know about Abraham from the Bible, the holy book for the Christians.

Yes, the two names Ibrahim and Abraham look alike; that is because Ibrahim is an Arabic name and Abraham is an English name; but it is the same man. The Bible tells us he is called a "friend of God" (Isaiah 41:8), and the Qur'an says he is a "friend of Allah" (Surah 4:125). So you can say he was a friend of the Almighty. Both books tell us about this friend; not only about him, but also about the Almighty who made the world and all beautiful things on it for the people.

Let us read together what both books tell us.

Note: The text of *Abraham and Ibrahim* is positioned on the pages to reflect the sources. The text on the left is from the Bible, the text on the right is from the Qur'an, and the text in the middle is from both.

The First Stories

Unit 1

The Creator and the Creation
(Genesis 1; Surahs 2:29–33; 41:10)

In many parts of the Qur'an you can read
about the Creator and the creation; and the
Bible says on the first page that God created
heaven and earth. God in Arabic is "Allah."

This is the beginning of the Bible:
God created the earth.
The earth was empty and without form.
It was very dark on the earth and the deep.
But the Spirit of God floated above.
And God said, "Let there be light," and the
   light appeared.
God saw that it was good,
so God divided the light from the darkness.
Only God knows how much time it really took,
because there was nothing on earth
to measure exactly when God was finished.

But, it says in the Bible and the Qur'an,
that for the Lord a thousand years is
   the same
as one day, and one day is the same as
   a thousand years
(Psalm 90:4; 2 Peter 3:8; Surah 32:5).

*In the Qur'an it even states that it could well
be fifty thousand years.*

We know now that the Lord counts in
   a different way than people do.
God's time is different.

> God stops God's working day when God wants to.

After the light and darkness were divided,
God made a division between heaven and earth
and between land and sea.
Then God said that there has to be green grass,
   young plants that give seeds, and fruit trees with fruit,
   fruit with seeds for new trees;

> and then God spoke: "Let it be" and it was so
> (Genesis 1:11–13; Surah 2:117).

The earth was covered with trees and plants with seeds
   for new trees and plants.
God saw what God had created was good.
Then God said that there has to be light in the sky,
so everything that lives and grows would know
the difference between day and night.
On God's word there came the sun
as a sign for the daytime, and the moon for
   the nighttime;
stars appeared in the sky to light the earth
and show the way by night.
And the sea?
God said that it has to be alive
with big and small sea animals,
lots and lots of fish big and small,
birds that fly around the earth and over the horizon.
The Lord blessed the birds, the fish, and the
   sea animals.
God made male and female and said,
"There is enough space to live in, so go and
   be plentiful."

> God did not only look after the sea,
> God also looked after the land. God spoke,
> "On this earth there have to be living
>   things, there have to be different sorts of
>   animals, crawling ones, wild ones,
>   and cattle" (Genesis 1:20–25;
>   Surahs 24:45; 36:36).

> *The Qur'an tells us that the*
> *animal's body shall give us warmth,*

> *food, and drink. Horses, donkeys, and mules shall*
> *not only carry freight but you can also ride on them (Surah 16:5, 8).*

God created the wild animals
and cattle with their own nature, even the ones that crawl,
big and small ones.
God created male and female of all the animals.
The skies, earth, and seas were filled with them.
God saw it was good.
Then God said,
"And now we will make human beings;
they will be like us and resemble us;
they will care for the fish, the birds, the cattle,
yes, for the whole world with all the animals."

> *It is written in the Qur'an (Surah 112:4)*
> *that no one or thing looks like Allah (God),*
> *but it says that Allah spoke to the angels and said*
> *that Allah was going to create a human who would look after the world*
> *instead of Allah (Surah 2:30).*

God created the human as a man and a woman.
First the man was created.
God brought the man to the animals.
God explained the different varieties
with their different names,
and for every male animal there was a female.
The Bible tells us it was then that the man knew
he was on his own and he had nobody;
he was lonely.
God did not like this either,
so God said,
"I will create a human companion for this man."
And God caused the man to sleep,
a deep long sleep;
God took one of the man's ribs,
covered the empty space with flesh,
and made a woman from the rib.
The Creator brought the woman to meet the man
and the man saw himself in her
and he was surprised.

Unit 1: The First Stories

He said: "The bones and flesh are the same as mine.
We are the same, a couple!"
So he called her "woman."

In Arabic she is Hawwa'.

These two people were blessed by God.
And God told them to be a couple and to
  be fruitful
and become a great people, so the world
  would be filled (Genesis 1:26–28;
  Surah 4:1).

When God saw that God's creation was completed
  and good,
God had a rest. The Lord blessed that day.
It was called a holy day, the day of rest.
It is a day for people to take a rest from their work
and to thank God for all things bright and beautiful
in creation (Genesis 2:1–3).
Many years later there was a psalm written about
  the creation.
A king wrote it.
His name was "David."

*In the Qur'an his name is "Dawud,"
and there he is called a prophet.*

He sang:
"O LORD, our Sovereign,
  how majestic is your name in
    all the earth!
When I look at your heavens,
    the work of your fingers,
  the moon and the stars that
    you have established;
what are human beings that you
    are mindful of them,
  mortals that you care for them?
Yet you have made them a little
    lower than God,
  and crowned them with glory
    and honor.
You have given them dominion
    over the works of your
    hands;

you have put all things under
  their feet,
all sheep and oxen,
  and also the beasts of the field,
the birds of the air, and the fish
  of the sea,
  whatever passes along the paths of the seas.
O LORD, our Sovereign,
  how majestic is your name in
    all the earth!" (Psalm 8:1a, 3–9).
This creation psalm is in the Bible.

The Qur'an tells us about the Creator:
Whatever is in Heaven and on the earth,
praise Allah!
For Allah is mighty and wise.
Allah has the rule over heaven and earth.
Allah gives life and takes life.
Allah is Almighty.
Allah is the First and the Last,
visible and invisible,
and Allah knows everything
(Surah 57:1–3).

Humankind
(Genesis 3; Surahs 7:11–25; 20:115–123)

Adam and Eve

    —in Arabic, Adam and Hawwa'—

were placed by God in the garden of Eden

    —Aden in the Qur'an.

The name of Adam means "man taken
    from soil,"
and Eve means "life,"
for she is the mother of humankind.
They were very happy to be in the garden.
A river flowed through the place.
All was green, growing, and flowering,
and the trees were bearing fruit for
    the couple.
The tree of everlasting life
stood in the middle of the garden,
as well as the tree that gives knowledge
of what is good and what is bad.
The fruit of the tree of knowledge was the
    only fruit
they were not allowed to eat.
If they did eat it, they would die.
But once a satan came.

    Previously the satan was an angel
    who quarreled with Allah; so Allah sent the
      angel away.
    Then this angel became a satan.
    The Qur'an says that this happened

Unit 1: The First Stories

> *when Allah created Adam; the satan didn't want to bow*
> *before this new creation.*

The Bible tells us that the satan came as a snake
and then said to Eve,
"Did God really tell you
not to eat fruit from any tree in the garden?"
"We may eat the fruit of any tree in the garden," the
   woman answered, "except the tree
that gives knowledge of what is good and what is bad.
If we eat its fruit, we will die."
The snake replied: "That's not true;
you will not die. God said so
because God knows that when you eat it
you will be like God,
knowing what is good and what is bad."
The woman saw how beautiful the tree was.
She trusted the snake and thought
how wonderful it would be
to become wise.
So she took some of the fruit and ate it.
Then she also gave some to her husband
and he also ate it.

> *In the Qur'an it is Adam*
> *to whom Satan whispered,*
> *"Shall I lead you to the tree of Eternity*
> *and to a kingdom that never decays?*
> *(Surah 20:120).*
> *Your Lord only forbade you this tree*
> *lest you should become angels*
> *or such beings as live forever" (Surah 7:20).*
> *And he swore to them both, that he was their*
>   *sincere adviser.*
> *So they tasted of the tree.*

As soon as they had eaten it
they saw that they were naked.

> Both books tell that they sewed leaves
>   together
> and covered themselves.

Then they hid from the Lord among the trees.
But the Almighty knows everything,

also what has happened in the garden.
In the Bible it is told that God called Adam,
"Adam, where are you?"
Adam replied from his hiding place,
"When I heard you coming I was afraid,
because I was naked."
"Who told you that you were naked?" the Lord
    answered.
"Did you eat the fruit
that I told you not to eat?"

> *"Didn't I forbid you this*
> *and didn't I warn you about Satan?"*
> *is the reply of Allah in the Qur'an (Surah 7:22).*

But Adam said to the Lord,
"The woman you put here with me
gave the fruit to me
and then I ate it."
The Lord asked the woman,
"Why did you do this?"
She replied: "The snake tricked me into eating it."
Then the Lord said to the snake,
"Because you have done so,
you will be punished for this;
you alone of all the animals must bear this curse,
that from now on, you will crawl on your belly,
and you will have to eat dust
 as long as you live.
I will put enmity between you and humankind.
Man will crush your head and you will bite his heel."
Then the Lord sent Adam out of the garden,
with Eve, to cultivate the soil
from which he had been formed.
Outside the garden they had to work hard
to survive, and their children were
 to be born with trouble and pain.

> *"Forgive us and have mercy upon us,"*
> *they begged (Surah 7:23).*
> *And the Almighty replied,*
> *"If you follow my guidance,*
> *you will not lose my way,*
> *nor fall into misery" (Surah 20:123).*
> *This prayer of man and woman*
> *and the promise of Allah (God)*

are the last words in the Qur'an about what happened in the garden of Aden (Eden).

The First Sons
(Genesis 4; Surah 5:27–32)

Outside the garden of Eden

—in the Qur'an, Aden—

life was totally different for Adam and Eve.
It was a life of heavy work, sorrows, and sadness.
But there was also happiness,
especially when their sons were born.
The first one was Cain
and the second one was Abel.

*In the Qur'an their names are not mentioned,
but Muslims call them Kabil and Habil.*

When they grew up, Cain became a farmer
and Abel became a shepherd.

After some time the two brothers brought
an offering to the Lord.
It is told in both holy books.

Cain brought some of his harvest
and gave it as an offering to the Lord.
Then Abel brought the first lamb
born to one of his sheep, killed it,
and gave the best parts of it
as an offering to the Lord.
The Lord accepted the offering of Abel,
but did not accept Cain's offering.
Cain got angry, but the Lord said to him,
"Why are you angry . . . ?
If you do well, will you not be accepted?
And if you don't do well,

sin is lurking at the door; its desire is for you,
but you should master it" (Genesis 4:6–7).
But Cain remained angry and he said to Abel,
"Let us go out to the field."

> *When they came into the field*
> *—so the Qur'an tells us—*
> *he said to his younger brother,*
> *"I will slay you."*
> *But the younger brother replied,*
> *"Even if you stretch out your hand to slay me,*
> *I will not slay you; for I fear Allah"*
> *(Surah 5:28).*

And Cain killed Abel.

Then the Lord said to Cain,
"Where is your brother Abel?"
Cain answered, "I do not know.
Am I my brother's keeper?"
But God said, "What have you done?
Your brother's blood is crying to me from the ground!
And now you are cursed from the ground,
which has opened its mouth
to receive your brother's blood from your hand.
When you till the ground, it will no longer
yield to you its strength.
You will be a fugitive and a wanderer on the earth"
   (Genesis 4:9–12).
Then Cain said to the Lord,
"Isn't my sin so great that I cannot bear
   the punishment?
Away from this land and away from your presence,
anyone who finds me will kill me."
"No," the Lord answered, "if anyone kills you,
seven lives will be taken in revenge."
So the Lord put a mark on Cain
to warn anyone who met him
not to kill him.
That's what the Bible tells us.

> *And because of this occurrence these words*
>   *of Allah*
> *are given in the Qur'an,*
> *"Therefore We ordained for the Israelites*
> *that if anyone killed a person*

> *who was not murdering others,*
> *it would be as if he killed*
> *the whole people;*
> *and if anyone saved a life,*
> *it would be as if he saved*
> *the life of the whole people (Surah 5:32).*

Then Cain went away from the presence of the Lord
and lived in the land of Nod,
east of Eden—the Bible tells us.
Adam and Eve had another son and
they called him Seth; it means "replacement."
"For God has appointed me another son to replace
 Abel," Eve said.
And still more children were born,
sons and daughters.
Seth also had children.
They were faithful to God.

Nuh/Noah
(Genesis 6—9; Surahs 7:59–63; 11:25–49; 71:1–28)

Years and years passed.
More and more people were living on
 the earth,
but less and less people were faithful
 to God.
They turned away from God
and made idols to serve them
instead of worshiping God.
The Lord was sorry that the Lord had
 made humankind.
The Lord said, "I will wipe out
these people I have created."
But the Lord was pleased with
 a few people;
one of them was Noah.

Nuh is his name in the Qur'an.
In that book he is called a prophet
with whom Allah has made a covenant.
Allah has sent Nuh with a message
to the idolaters of Wadd, Souwa,
Jaghut, Jawuk, and Masr to tell them,
"You have no other god but Allah.
So fear Allah; then Allah may forgive you
 your sins.
I fear for you the punishment of a terrible day."
Meanwhile Allah ordered Nuh to build a boat

(in the Bible it is called an ark).
Noah had to build it of good timber,
and to cover the ark with tar inside and out.
The ark must have a roof, decks, and doors in it
with rooms for all animals, male and female.

Unit 1: The First Stories

God gave all measurements of the boat to Noah
and God said,
"I am going to send a flood to destroy the earth."

> *The Qur'an gives the people's response*
> *to Nuh's warning.*
> *Their leaders said to him,*
> *"You are confused."*
> *But he replied: "I am not confused,*
> *but in the Name of Allah I give you good advice.*
> *Don't you wonder that there has come*
> *a reminder from your Lord*
> *through a man of your own people to warn you,*
> *so that you may fear Allah*
> *and may receive the Lord's mercy?"*
> *But the people accused Nuh of being a liar*
> *and they said, "Bring upon us what you*
> *threaten us with, if you speak the truth!"*
> *Nuh said: "Allah will bring it on you*
>   *if Allah wills,*
> *and then you will not be able to stop it!"*

When the ark was ready,

> God told Noah to go into the ark
> with his wife and with his sons,

Shem, Ham, and Japheth, their wives,
 and all kinds of animals.
God closed the door,
and the sky burst open,
and water from beneath and rains from above
filled up the earth for forty days and nights.
As the water rose,
the boat began to float.
Above the mountains the water rose,
and above the mountains the ark was raised up
   by the water.

> *In the Qur'an it is mentioned that another son*
>   *of Nuh*
> *didn't want to go into the ark. He said:*
> *"I will find a high mountain that protects me*
>   *against the water."*
> *But he was drowned (Surah 11:42–43).*

After forty days and forty nights the rain stopped.
The Lord caused a wind to blow
and slowly the water went down
together with the ark.
After one hundred and fifty days

        the ark came to rest upon a mountain;

Ararat is its name in the Bible

        and Judi in the Qur'an (Surah 11:44).

Slowly the tops of the mountains
rose up from the water
and the mountains became visible again.
It took weeks and weeks
before Noah could open a window.
He sent out a raven
and the raven flew to and fro
until the water was completely gone.
Then Noah sent out a dove,
but the dove didn't find food
and flew back to the ark.
One week later Noah sent the dove out again;
it returned to him in the evening
with a fresh olive leaf in its beak.
So Noah knew that the water had gone down.
Then he waited another seven days
and sent the dove out once more;
this time it didn't come back.
Then Noah removed the covering from the boat.
He looked around and saw
that the ground was getting dry.
When it was completely dry,

        God allowed Noah to go out of the ark
        with his wife and children
        and with all animals;
        both books tell us so.

Outside the ark Noah built an altar to the Lord
and offered burnt offerings on the altar
to thank God.
And God made a covenant with Noah and
   his descendants,

and with all animals
that came out of the ark.
This is the covenant:
that never again would all living beings
be destroyed by a flood.
And God said,
"I have set my bow in the clouds, and it shall
be a sign of the covenant between me and the earth.
When the bow is in the clouds, I will see it and
remember the covenant that is between me and
you and every living creature of all flesh;
and the waters shall never again become
a flood to destroy all flesh" (Genesis 9:13–15).

*In the Qur'an, Nuh is mentioned
together with Ibrahim, Musa, 'Isa,
and Muhammad.
They are called prophets with whom Allah
has made
a covenant (Surah 33:7).*

Abraham, or Ibrahim, lived after Noah.
The next story tells us more about Abraham.

Unit 2

Ibrahim/ Abraham

Ibrahim/Abraham
(Genesis 11:22–32; 12:1–9; Surah 21:51–71)

Noah lived to be very old.
His household grew into a large family.
He saw his grandchildren and great-grandchildren
   grow up.
The Bible lists many names of Noah's offspring
up to the name of Abraham.

In the Qur'an his name is Ibrahim.

Who was that man?
He was the son of Terah
and the grandson of Nahor,
who was a descendant of Noah's son Shem.
The name of Abraham's wife was Sarah.
Abraham and Sarah had no children,
but God promised Abraham offspring,
as countless as the stars in the sky.
They first had to go on a journey.
God said to Abraham that he had to leave
his father's house and his country,
to go to the land that God was going to show him.

*In the Qur'an it is written
that Ibrahim left his country
because the people did wrong things.
They made idols and bowed down to them;
this is called "shirk."
Even Ibrahim's father did so.
Therefore, Ibrahim destroyed all idols,
except the biggest one.
When the people asked Ibrahim,
"Is it you who did this to our gods?" he said,*

Unit 2: Ibrahim/Abraham

> "Nay, this was done by the biggest one.
>   Ask him!"
> This put the people to shame,
> because they knew very well
> that a statue cannot speak.
> Finally they said to Ibrahim,
> "You know that such a statue can't talk."
> Then he replied,
> "So, instead of Allah, you worship
> something that helps you in no way?
> Do you have no sense?"
> This made the people angry
> and they wanted to set Ibrahim on fire.
> But Allah saved him from the fire
> and sent him away from these people,
> the Qur'an tells us.

Then this descendant of Noah,
together with his wife, Sarah, and his
  nephew, Lot

—Lut in the Qur'an—

moved to the land promised by God.

Ibrahim and Lut/ Abraham and Lot
(Genesis 13—18; 19:1–29; Surahs 26:160–173; 11:70–83)

The Bible tells us that Abraham
went to the country of Canaan.
He arrived in the city of Shechem.
And God said to Abraham,
"This is the country that I am going
to give to your descendants.
And through you I will bless all the nations."
Then Abraham built there an altar to God.
Thereafter he moved on to a city called Bethel.
There he built another altar and worshiped God.
And God blessed Abraham and his family
with so many cattle that the grass and the water
were no longer enough for all his and Lot's animals.
So the shepherds ran into trouble.
Abraham said to Lot,
"It is not good that our shepherds have troubles,
because we are relatives.
So let us separate and spread out our living places,
as the land is large enough.
If you go to the north, I'll go to the south;
and if you want to go to the south,
I'll go to the north."
Lot chose the region of the river Jordan,
with its green prairies.
Near Sodom and Gomorrah he set up his camp
on the beautiful ground.
But the people of these cities were wicked
and sinned against the Lord.
And where did Abraham go?
Abraham stayed in the land of Canaan
and settled near Hebron;

Unit 2: Ibrahim/Abraham

there he built another altar to the Lord.
God said to him,
"Look carefully in all directions;
I am going to give all the land as far as you can see it
to you and to all your countless descendants."
And God promised Abraham a son
with whom God would make a covenant forever.
Some time later Ishmael was born;

in the Qur'an his name is Isma'il.

Abraham and Sarah had no children yet,
so Abraham asked God to make that covenant
with Ishmael. But God said,
"Surely, I will bless Ishmael, as you are his father.
He will be the father of twelve princes
and I will make a great nation of his descendants.
I will establish my covenant
with the son born to you and Sarah, Isaac,
as we agreed."
And God's token of the covenant
was the circumcision of all males from eight days old
who lived with Abraham,
including Ishmael and Abraham himself.
And how did Lot do in Sodom?
He found a wife; they married,
and two daughters were born.
But a war began in that beautiful place.
Kings of big cities fought against
kings of other big cities.
The king of Sodom lost
and all people in that town were captured
by the winning kings.
Lot and his wife and daughters were also taken.
But a man escaped and reported all this to Abraham.
Then Abraham called all the fighting men in his camp,
pursued with them the enemies, attacked them,
and rescued Lot, the women, all other prisoners
and the loot that had been taken.
When Abraham returned,
Melchizedek brought bread and wine to him.
He was the king of Salem
and also a priest of the Most High God,
the Bible tells us.
Melchizedek blessed Abraham in the name of God.

And Abraham gave a tenth of all the loot
to Melchizedek.
But the men of Sodom and Gomorrah
still sinned against God
and didn't want to do God's will.

> *The Qur'an says that Allah made Lot a prophet,*
> *and told him to warn the people.*
> *But the men of Sodom accused him of being a liar*
> *and they said that they would expel him from*
> *the city (Surah 26:161–167).*

> They continued sinning until
> it was too late for them.
> Then two messengers came to visit Lot.
> They told him that in the name of God
> he must leave that place,
> because God was going to punish the city.

The men of the city came to know this
and wanted to do evil things to the visitors.
They would have attacked Lot,
but the visitors pulled him back into the house,
shut the door, and struck all the men outside
 with blindness,
so that they couldn't find the door.

> Then the two visitors told Lot to leave the
> city with his wife, daughters, and
> sons-in-law, before sunrise.

But Lot's sons-in-law didn't want to go with him;
they thought that he was joking.

> Then the two men urged Lot and his family,
> "Run for your lives! Don't look back!"
> But Lot's wife looked back

and she was turned into a pillar of salt,
the Bible tells us.

> *In the Qur'an it was already predicted*
> *that the woman would not be saved;*
> *she lingered behind and was struck*
> *by a shower of brimstone.*

Unit 2: Ibrahim/Abraham

> *The Qur'an calls her an old woman*
> *(Surahs 26:171; 37:135).*

> The next morning God destroyed the cities of
> Sodom and Gomorrah with fire.

When Abraham came out of his camp and saw the fire,
he remembered the message of the visitors.
They had visited Abraham before going to Lot.
He had offered them a meal and they had explained
 to him
the plan to destroy both cities.
Afterward they went up to Lot in Sodom.
A third visitor stayed with Abraham
to tell him what would happen with the city.

> Abraham again and again asked God to
> save the city,
> because Lot and his family lived there.

And repeatedly he was told
that God would do so
if fifty or forty innocent people were found, or
even if it was only thirty or twenty people
(for Abraham reduced the number every time).
Finally, he asked what God would do
if only ten innocents were found;
and he was told that even then
the city would be saved.
But he was not allowed to ask again.
So when that morning he looked out
and saw the fire from afar, he understood
that not even ten innocent people
could be found in Sodom and Gomorrah.

> He also had heard a good message from
> his visitors.
> It was their promise that next year
> Sarah would bear a son.
> In the Qur'an and the Bible it is written
> that Abraham's wife could hardly believe it,
> as she was very old already.
> But in both books it is also written
> that for the Lord nothing is impossible
> (Genesis 18:14; Surah 11:72–73).

The Sons of Ibrahim/Abraham
(Genesis 21—22; Surah 37:102–107)

One year later a son was born to Abraham and Sarah.
His name is Isaac

    —in the Qur'an, Ishak.

  In both books we can read that, one night
  in a dream, the Almighty ordered Abraham
  to offer his son as a sacrifice.

In the Bible, Isaac is mentioned;

    in the Qur'an, Isma'il is intended,
    although his name is not mentioned. When his
    son was old enough to work with his father,
    Ibrahim said, "My son, I have seen myself
    sacrifice you in a dream. What do you think?"
    He said, "Father, do as you are commanded
    and, God willing, you will find me steadfast"
    (Surah 37:102–103).

  Happily this ended well.
  God saw Abraham willing to obey God
  and this was sufficient to God. The Lord
   stopped him.
  Then, when Abraham raised his eyes
  he saw a ram caught by the horns in a bush.
  And Abraham thankfully offered the ram
   to God
  instead of his son.

Unit 2: Ibrahim/Abraham

> *The Muslims celebrate this event every year.*
> *A ram or other animal*
> *is slaughtered and the meat is*
> *shared with the family, friends, and the poor.*
> *In the Arabic language this feast*
> *is called 'Id-al-Adha.*

Much happened in the lives of the
two sons of Abraham.
The Bible tells us that Ishmael had been living
with his small brother Isaac for a few years.
But then Sarah wanted him to leave
with his mother.
That became a time of great sadness.
Ishmael almost perished with thirst
on the long way through the desert.
But God protected Hagar and her son.
God sent an angel to her to show a well;

> *the Arabic name of this well is Zamzam.*

God also gave Hagar
a dwelling place in the desert of Paran;
there she could stay with Ishmael.
And once again God promised Hagar
that God would give many children to her son,
so that they would become a great nation.
Ishmael became a skilful hunter.
Although he was now living far away from his father,
Abraham didn't forget him.
For Ishmael was his son, wasn't he?

> *In the Qur'an it is written*
> *that father and son together*
> *built a house for the Lord*
> *in Ismai'l's new dwelling place.*
> *It is the Ka'ba, in Makkah, or Mecca.*
> *In that place Ibrahim prayed to Allah*
> *for himself and for both of his sons.*
> *"O my Lord!" he said, "make this city*
> *a city of peace and security;*
> *and preserve me and my sons*
> *from worshiping idols.*
> *Because they indeed lead many people astray"*
> *(Surah 14:35–41).*

The Sons of Ibrahim/Abraham

The Lord heard Ibrahim's prayer;
Allah sanctified the newly built house
and made of it a place of worship
and sacrifice.
And much later Allah sent the angel Jabra'il
with messages for the descendants of Isma'il,
especially to one of them called Muhammad.
Muhammad was to give these messages to
   his people;
therefore Allah called him a "prophet."
All these messages were written down in a book;
it became the Holy Qur'an,
full of words through Jabra'il to Muhammad
in the Name of Allah,
and full of memories of the past:
the time of Ibrahim, Isma'il, Ishak, and Ya'kub
and all other believers.

Warnings and guidelines are also given
in that book, as are given in the Bible,
the book of the descendants of Ishak.
And like the Bible, the Qur'an also delivers
the most important message, that the Lord
   Almighty is one,
and that there is no god but Allah,
the Creator, the Eternal,
the First and the Last,
the Light of heaven and earth
(Surahs 57:3; 24:35; see Revelation 22:13).

Right up to today these words are being read
   and told
to the descendants; also about the Ka'ba,
the house of the Lord in Mecca.
And many Muslims still go on pilgrimage
to that place, at least once in their lives.
And if the journey is too expensive,
or people are very poor,
then sometimes they collect money
to send one member of their family
or one inhabitant of their village
to Mecca, on behalf of all.

The Sons of Isma'il/Ishmael and Ishak/Isaac

(Genesis 21—22; Surah 37:102–107)

Ishmael grew in length and strength.
His mother found an Egyptian wife for him,
the Bible tells us.
They got married and, in the years after that,
twelve sons and at least one daughter were born.
She was called Mahalath, or Basemath
(Genesis 25:12–17).
Later, this daughter was married to a son of Isaac.
The sons lived east of Egypt
and became ancestors of their tribes.

> *In the Qur'an it is written that Isma'il was true*
> *to what he promised, and that he taught*
>   *his people*
> *how to pray and how to share with the poor.*
> *Therefore Allah called him a messenger*
> *and a prophet (Surah 19:54–55).*

Isaac also grew into an adult,
and his father Abraham wanted to find a good wife
    for him.
Abraham felt too old to do this himself,
so he sent his oldest servant, Eliezer,
to his old country
where his relatives were still living.
Perhaps Eliezer could find among them a woman
who would agree to marry Isaac.
He found Rebecca, and after some days
he was allowed to take her to Isaac.
When Isaac saw her, he loved her (Genesis 24).

They married and twins were born,
Esau and Jacob.
Later it was Esau who married Mahalath,
the daughter of Ishmael (Genesis 28:8–9).
About Ishmael the Bible also tells us
that when Abraham died,
Ishmael and Isaac together
buried their father in the cave of Machpelah,
the place where Abraham's wife, Sarah, was also
    buried (Genesis 25).
Much later, after Rebecca had died
and Isaac's life had also come to an end,
he also was buried, like his wife,
in the cave of Machpelah,
by his twin sons, Esau and Jacob (Genesis 35:28).

Esau had five sons, Jacob twelve,
and both had daughters (Genesis 29—30).
Both families increased so much
and had so many cattle
that they could no longer live together.
Therefore, Esau and his family went to another place.
The brothers parted in peace from each other.
That was better than in the past,
when they were still younger.
At that time there was trouble between them
about which of the two was most important
and would inherit the greater part of
their father Isaac's heritage.
Then Jacob ran away from his father's house,
as he had cheated his father
and his brother, and Esau wanted to kill Jacob
because of that.
This is told to us in the Bible.
In spite of that, God promised Jacob that God would be
    with him on his way.
And the Lord gave a new name to Jacob: "Israel"
(Genesis 32:22–29).
Many years later, before Isaac died,
the two brothers met again.
They hugged and kissed each other.
So all fear and all anger was wiped away (Genesis 33).
This is what reconciliation means.

Unit 3
Ya'kub/Jacob

The Sons of Ya'kub/Jacob
(Genesis 37—50; Surah 12)

Much is written about Jacob,
in the Qur'an as well as in the Bible.

> *In the Qur'an his name is Ya'kub.*

Both books tell us about his twelve sons,
especially about one of them.
Joseph was his name;

> *in the Qur'an his name is Yusef.*

He was the eleventh of the twelve sons of Jacob,
and the eldest of Rachel's two sons.
Rachel was already dead.
Jacob spoiled Joseph; he made a beautiful robe for him.
Joseph brought bad reports to his father
about what his brothers were doing.

> He also had some dreams;
> in the dreams it seemed
> that his father and brothers bowed for him.
> He told his father and his brothers this.

>> *"Oh my father, I dreamt that I saw eleven stars
>>   and the sun and the moon. I saw them
>> bow down to me." His father warned him
>> not to tell his brothers,
>> and to leave the interpretation to Allah,
>> the Qur'an tells us (Surah 12:5).*

But Joseph's brothers had already heard it
and they got angry, the Bible says.

Unit 3: Ya'kub/Jacob

> They wanted to rid themselves of this
> proud Joseph.
> And once, when all were far from home,
> they attacked him and threw him
> into a deep, dry well.

And as they were considering
whether or not to kill him,
they saw a caravan of traders
coming from Gilead and
traveling on the way to Egypt.

> *In the Qur'an the name of that country is Misr.*

They were Ishmaelites and Midianites;
those are descendants of Abraham and Hagar
and of Abraham and Keturah, whom he married
after Sarah's death (Genesis 25).
Joseph's brothers decided
it was better to sell Joseph than to kill him.
So they pulled him out of the well
and sold him for twenty pieces of silver,
the Bible tells us.

> *According to the Qur'an, the merchants themselves*
> *pulled Yusef out of the well.*
> *For their water carrier let his bucket down*
> *into the well to get water.*
> *Instead of water, he found a boy in the well*
> *and called: "Good news! A young man is in*
>   *the well!"*
> *So the merchants concealed him as a treasure.*
> *But then the brothers came along*
> *and wanted to be paid for Yusef.*
> *For a few dirhams he was sold,*
> *the Qur'an tells us (Surah 12:19–20).*

Then the brothers told their father Jacob
that a wild animal had killed Joseph;

> *a wolf, the Qur'an says.*

They showed him Joseph's robe,
after having dipped it into a goat's blood.
And Jacob mourned his son for many years,
so it is written in both books.

Yusef/Joseph in Egypt
(Genesis 39—41; Surah 12:21–57)

In Egypt

   —"Misr" in the Qur'an—

Joseph was sold to one of Pharaoh's officers;

in the Bible his name is Potiphar.

Joseph lived in Potiphar's house.
The Lord Almighty blessed Joseph
and gave him wisdom, both books tell us.
So Joseph made the right decisions
and Potiphar saw that the Lord was
   with Joseph
and he was pleased with him.
Potiphar made him his personal servant.
Potiphar's wife also saw that he was a
   good man.
She fell in love with him
 and wanted him to fall in love with her.
But Joseph said that he didn't want to
do wicked things toward the Lord
and toward her husband.
And when she couldn't tempt him,
she had him imprisoned by lying.
However, even in prison, the Lord took care
   of him
and gave him wisdom. Joseph saw this
when the Pharaoh's wine steward and the
   chief baker were put in prison.
Something wrong had taken place in the palace
and because of that, both men were punished,

Unit 3: Ya'kub/Jacob

so is written in both books.
Then, one night each man had a dream.
The wine steward said,
"In my dream there was a grapevine
with three branches on it.
I took the ripe grapes and squeezed them
into the king's cup and I gave it to him."
The chief baker also told his dream to Joseph,
"I was carrying three bread baskets on
   my head.
In the top basket there were all kinds of
pastries for the king, and the birds were
   eating them."
What could be the meaning of these dreams?

> *Then Yusef first told about the faith*
> *of his ancestors Ibrahim, Ishak, and Ya'kub,*
> *their faith in Allah, the only God to be worshiped,*
> *the Qur'an says (Surah 12:38–40).*

Speaking about the dreams, Joseph said,
"It is only God who grants the ability to
   interpret dreams:
The three branches in the wine steward's
   dream
represent three days. In three days you will
   give the king
his cup, as you did before.
Please remember me and be kind enough
to mention me to the king
and help me to get out of this prison,
when everything is going well for you.
The three baskets of the chief baker
also represent three days.
In three days you will be killed
and the birds will eat you."
And so it happened.
But the wine steward, the one who
   was released,
forgot what he had promised to Joseph.
He remembered only two years later.
That was at the time that Pharaoh

—*Fir'awn in the Qur'an*—

Yusef/Joseph in Egypt

had dreams one night.
Both books tell about it.
In the first dream, he saw seven fat cows.
The fat cows were being eaten by seven
   thin cows.
Then he dreamt again and saw
seven ears of grain, full and ripe.
Then seven other ears of grain sprouted,
thin and scorched by the desert wind;
and the thin ears of grain swallowed the
   full ones.
Pharaoh woke up and was worried.
He sent for all the wise men of Egypt
and told them his dreams,
but no one could explain them to him.
Then the wine steward remembered Joseph
and he said to Pharaoh,
"I must confess today that I have
   done wrong,"
and he told the king about his own dream,
about Joseph's interpretation
and how things turned out just as Joseph
   had said.
So Pharaoh sent for Joseph.

> *In the Qur'an it is written*
> *that Yusef refused to go along with him,*
> *until the woman who had lied*
> *about him told the truth.*
> *Potiphar's wife told him*
> *that she had tried to tempt Yusef,*
> *but he had remained honest.*
> *When Yusef heard this, he was glad to see*
> *that Allah rewarded honesty*
> *(Surah 12:50–52).*

Now he could go to the king with
   God's help.
He was shaved and dressed
and then taken to Pharaoh.
Both books tell us so.
The king said to Joseph, "It is said about you,
that you only need to hear what I dreamt
to be able to interpret it."
But Joseph replied, "It is not I;
only the Lord can give the interpretation."

Unit 3: Ya'kub/Jacob

> Then Pharaoh told his dreams
> and Joseph explained what they meant.
> He said, "By means of these dreams God
>   has revealed
> what God is going to do.
> The seven fat cows and the seven full ears
>   of grain mean
> that seven years of a great harvest will
>   come first.
> The seven thin cows
> and the seven thin and scorched ears of
>   grain mean
> that after the seven good years
> seven years of famine will come.
> So both dreams have the same meaning
> and the reason for dreaming twice is
> that it will surely happen.
> Therefore, you must appoint some officials
> to collect a fifth of the crops
> during the seven years of plenty,
> to store it up in the cities and to guard it.
> The food will be a reserve supply for
>   the country
> during the seven years of famine that are
>   going to befall Egypt."
> Pharaoh approved this plan.
> He trusted Joseph and said to his officials,
> "We will never find a better man than he,
> a man who has God's spirit in him."
> So Pharaoh appointed him governor over
>   all Egypt.

He removed from his finger the ring
engraved with the royal seal
and put it on Joseph's finger.
He also gave him a wife, Asenath,
the daughter of the priest Potiphera.
Joseph traveled all over the land.
During seven years of plenty he stored in every city
the food collected from the fields around.

The Sons of Ya'kub/Jacob Go to Egypt

(Genesis 42—45; Surah 12:58–98)

After those seven good years
the seven years of famine came,
not only in Egypt but also in Canaan,
the country where Jacob and his family lived.
Jacob was afraid there would not be
enough food for all his children and grandchildren.

> When he heard that grain was being sold
>   in Egypt,
> he sent ten sons to that country,
> both books tell us.
> When they arrived at the palace of Pharaoh
>
> —in the Qur'an "Fir'awn"—
>
> they left behind their donkeys
> and bowed down before the governor of the
>   land of Egypt,
> who was selling grain.
> They didn't know that he was their brother,
> but Joseph immediately recognized
>   his brothers.
> When they were bowing down
> with their faces to the ground,
> he remembered his dreams they had denied.

He acted as if he didn't know them
and asked them harshly,
"Where do you come from?"
They answered, "We have come from Canaan
to buy food." But he said,

43

Unit 3: Ya'kub/Jacob

"You are spies; you have come
to find out where our country is weak."
Then the ten men told him the story of their family,
"We were twelve brothers in all,
sons of the same man in Canaan.
One brother has died
and the youngest is now with our father."
But they didn't get away with that story.
Again the governor accused them of being spies,
and he detained them for some days.
And as proof of telling the truth, he kept one of them
    in Egypt,
while the others had to go for their youngest brother,
otherwise they could not buy any more grain.

> *In the Qur'an it is written that Yusef said,*
> *"Don't you see that I give you a full measure*
> *of grain and the best hospitality?*
> *But if you don't bring your youngest brother to me,*
> *you shall have no grain,*
> *nor shall you come near me" (Surah 12:59–60).*

After having ordered this, Joseph heard
his brothers talking among themselves,
"Now we are being punished
for what we did to Joseph.
For we saw the great trouble he was in
when he begged for help, but we would not listen.
That's why we are now in trouble."
The brothers didn't know that the governor
could understand their language.
Reuben, the oldest, said to the others,
"I told you not to harm the boy,
but you wouldn't listen.
And now we are paying for his death."
Joseph left them and began to cry.
When he was able to speak, he came back,
picked out Simeon and bound him.
Nine brothers went home with the grain
and with the order to bring Benjamin with them
next time.

> Joseph had secretly given orders to
>   his servants
> to put back in each man's sack his money

The Sons of Ya'kub/Jacob Go to Egypt

> —his "stock-in-trade" the Qur'an says.
> Yusef hoped that this
> might cause his brothers to come back,
> this book tells us.

When, on the way home, the brothers
found their money in the top of their sacks,
they were very upset.

> *The Qur'an says they were happy. They said,*
> *"Father, we need no more to trade.*
> *We will be entitled to an extra measure so*
> *easily achieved.*

They thought that God Almighty had done
  this to them.
When they got home, they sadly told their
  old father
all that had happened.
And they entreated him to allow them
to take Benjamin to the governor next time.
But Jacob said,
"You rob me of children.

Joseph is gone, Simeon is gone
and now you want to take Benjamin away.
He shall not go!
Something might happen to him on the way.
I am an old man, and the sorrow you would cause me
would kill me. Why did you tell that man
that you had another brother?"
The sons answered,
"The man kept asking about us and our family:
'Is your father still living?
Do you have other brothers?'
We had to answer his questions.
How could we know that he would tell us
to bring our brother with us?"
But when the famine in Canaan intensified
and Jacob's family had eaten
all the grain they brought from Egypt,
he considered permitting his sons
to take Benjamin with them to the governor.

> *In the Qur'an, Ya'kub says,*
> *"Shall I trust you with him with any result*

Unit 3: Ya'kub/Jacob

*other than when I trusted you
with his brother the last time?
Never will I send him with you
unless you swear a solemn oath to me,
in Allah's name,
that you will be sure to bring him back to me."
The brothers swore.
And they convinced their father, saying,
"Now we will get another full camel's load."
Ya'kub agreed.
"But enter not all by one gate," he said.
"Enter by different gates."
They did so, although it was not necessary,
as Allah took care of them
and nobody could interfere,
so it is written in the Qur'an.*

Jacob sent the best products of the land
in his sons' packs as a present for the governor:
resin, honey, spices, pistachio nuts and almonds
and also twice as much money,
because of what was returned in the top of their sacks.
Finally he gave them his son Benjamin.
So eleven sons arrived in Egypt.
When Joseph saw his younger brother coming with
    his brothers,
he said to the housemaster,
"Take these men to my house.
They are going to eat with me at noon;
so prepare the meal."
But the brothers were not happy
to be in the governor's house;
they were afraid, because of that money,
and they told the housemaster this.
In the meantime, they put down
the presents from their father;
but the housemaster said,
"Don't worry and don't be afraid.
Your God must have put the money in your sacks
    for you.
I received your payment."
When the brothers saw how they had been seated
    at the table
in the order of their age from the eldest to the youngest,
they looked at one another in amazement.

The Sons of Ya'kub/Jacob Go to Egypt

And Benjamin was served five times as much
as the others.

> Meanwhile, Joseph ordered the housemaster
> to fill the men's sacks with grain
> and to put each man's money in the top
>   of his sack.
> Moreover, the governor's silver cup was
>   to be put
> in the youngest man's sack,
> both books say.
> When the brothers had gone only a
>   short distance
> from the city, Joseph said to his housekeeper:
> "Hurry after those men and ask them,
> why they have stolen the silver cup of
>   the governor."
> Again, the brothers were frightened,
> but then they got angry and said,
> "What do you mean, sir, by talking like this?
> We swear that we have done no such thing.
> You know that we brought back to you
> the money we found in the top of our sacks.
> If anyone of us is found to have it,
> he will be put to death."

>> "The penalty will be the enslavement of the
>> person in whose bag the cup is found"
>> (Surah 2:75).

> The housekeeper searched carefully
> and the cup was found in Benjamin's sack.
> Upset, the brothers returned to the city.
> Back in the governor's house, they
>   bowed down
> before him and Joseph said,
> "What have you done? Didn't you know
> that a man in my position could find you out?"
> Then Judah rose up and pleaded in favor of
>   his old father.
> The father had not been willing
> to send his youngest son with them
> as his other son had already perished,
> but he did it because the governor wanted
>   him to do so.

Unit 3: Ya'kub/Jacob

If the young boy did not come home,
his old father would die.

> And Judah proposed that, instead,
> he himself would stay with the governor
>   as his slave.
> Then Joseph was no longer able to control
>   his feelings.
> He sent away all his servants and said,
> "I am Joseph. Is my father still alive?"
> The brothers were so terrified
> that they could not answer.
> But Joseph told them to come closer
> and not to be upset.
> Both books mention Joseph's words
> that, although they sold him to Egypt,
> it was really the Almighty who sent him
> ahead of them to save people's lives.

> *The Qur'an tells us that Yusef*
> *had already told his younger brother*
> *that he was his brother Yusef*
> *and that he would take care*
> *that nothing bad would happen to the boy.*
> *It is also written that when the cup was found*
> *in the youngest brother's sack,*
> *the boy himself stayed with Yusef*
> *and only the others were sent home.*
> *It was Yusef's hope that if he did this,*
> *his father would come to Egypt.*
> *And that is what happened.*
> *The Qur'an also tells us*
> *the words of the brothers to Yusef,*
> *"By Allah! Indeed, Allah has preferred you*
> *   above us,*
> *and we certainly have been guilty of sin!"*
> *(Surah 12:91).*

Ya'kub/Jacob in Egypt
(Genesis 46—50; Surah 12:99–101)

The Bible tells us that the Pharaoh

—*Fir'awn in the Qur'an*—

told Joseph to give wagons to his brothers
for their wives and the small children
and to have their father come with them.
He also ordered them to load their animals with grain,
bread, and other food for the journey,
as well as a change of clothes.
Benjamin even got five outfits
and three hundred pieces of silver.
Ten donkeys were loaded with the best Egyptian goods.
Then Joseph sent his brothers off and said,
"Don't quarrel on the way!"
When they came home, the sons told their father
the good news that Joseph was still alive
and that he had invited his father to come to Egypt
with his family.

> *They had taken with them one of Yusef's shirts;*
> *they cast it over his face*
> *and Yakub regained his sight,*
> *the Qur'an tells us.*
> *And on the way he said,*
> *"I do indeed sense the presence of Yusef!"*

In a dream—the Bible tells us—
God said to Jacob,
"Don't be afraid to go to Egypt;
I will make your descendants a great nation there;
I will go with you to Egypt.

Unit 3: Ya'kub/Jacob

Surely, I will bring your descendants back to this land,
And Joseph will be with you when you die."
Jacob arrived in Egypt in safety
with all his family and all his cattle.

> *The Qur'an tells us*
> *how Yusef welcomed his family.*
> *He provided a home for them with himself*
> *and raised them high on the throne.*
> *But they bowed deeply to him.*
> *Then Yusef said to his father, "O my father, this*
>   *is the fulfillment*
> *of my vision of old!*
> *Allah has made it come true!*
> *Allah took me out of prison*
> *and brought you all here out of the desert!"*

Joseph took his father and five of his brothers
to Pharaoh and introduced them, the Bible tells us.
Jacob blessed Pharaoh;
and Pharaoh gave Jacob the best part of the land
in the region of Goshen
for his family and his cattle.
And he said, "If there are any capable men
   among them,
put them in charge of my own livestock."
Jacob lived in Egypt for seventeen years.
When the time drew near for him to die,
he called his sons, one by one.
He blessed them,
beginning with Joseph and his two sons,
Manasseh and Ephraim.
The younger one was blessed first.

> *The Qur'an mentions the last sayings*
> *of Ya'kub with his sons,*
> *"What will you worship after me?"*
> *They said, "We shall worship Allah,*
> *your Lord and the Lord of your forefathers*
>   *Ibrahim, Isma'il, and Ishak,*
> *the Only True One; to Allah we submit"*
> *(Surah 2:133).*

Then Jacob lay down and he died.
Joseph and his brothers and all relatives
carried his body to Canaan.

All Pharaoh's officials and the leading men of Egypt
went with Joseph, in chariots and on horseback.
In Canaan they buried the body of Jacob
in the cave at Machpelah, the same place
where also his ancestors were buried,
the Bible tells us.
Now that their father had died,
the sons themselves came to Joseph.
They bowed down for him and said,
"Before your father died, he told us to ask you,
'Please forgive us the wrong that we have done.'"
Joseph cried and he said,
"I can't put myself in the place of God.
You plotted evil against me, but God turned
   it into good,
in order to preserve the lives of many people
who are alive today because of what happened.
You have nothing to fear.
I will take care of you and your children."
And Joseph did so unto his death.

> *In the Qur'an, the story of Yusef*
> *is not called a story, but a confirmation*
> *of what happened;*
> *a detailed exposition of all things,*
> *and a guide and comfort to those who believe*
> *(Surah 12:111).*

Musa/Moses

Unit 4

The Birth of Musa/Moses
(Exodus 1—2:10; Surah 28:1–13)

Joseph's family lived in Egypt for a long time.
Many children were born,
so the family grew into a large nation;
"Israel" is its name, given by the Almighty.
But a new Pharaoh

—*Fir'awn in the Qur'an*—

who came to power in Egypt
knew nothing about Jacob and Joseph.

> He only thought,
> "This nation is greater than our own people.
> When their men choose to join our enemies
> in case of a war, Egypt will lose."
> Therefore he made a plan to prevent
> the Hebrew people from becoming strong.
> He gave them slave labor to do and
>   made them work very hard;
> and they were beaten and maltreated by
>   slave drivers.
> But the more the slave drivers did so,
> the stronger the Israelites became
> and the more children were born.
> Then Pharaoh ordered every newborn boy
> to be thrown into the Nile, a broad river.
> Both books tell us so.
> But some parents hid their little boys.
> Amram

—*'Imran in the Qur'an*—

and his wife Jochebed did so, as they saw
that their little son was a fine baby.
When they could no longer hide him,
they made a basket for him,
covered it with tar to made it watertight,
put their baby in it, and placed it in the
   tall grass
at the edge of the river.
The baby's sister stood some distance away
to see what would happen to him.

The princess came down to the place
to take a bath in the Nile
and she noticed the basket.
When she opened it she saw a baby boy.
He began to cry and she felt sorry for him.

"This is one of the Hebrew babies," she said
and she wanted to take him with her.

*In the Qur'an, it is Pharaoh's wife who rescues him.
Pharaoh's daughter is not mentioned.*

At that moment, his sister appeared and said,
"Shall I go and call a Hebrew woman
to nurse the child for you?"
And when the woman agreed,
the girl called the baby's own mother.
Pharaoh's daughter (wife in the Qur'an)
   said to her,
"Take this baby and nurse him for me,
and I will pay you."
So she took her baby and nursed him.
Later, when he was old enough,
she took him to Pharaoh's house.

The king's daughter adopted him as her own son
and called him Moses;
it means "pulled out of the water."

Moses grew into a remarkable man.
Both books tell us about him.

*In the Qur'an his name is Musa; that's Arabic.
This book also mentions Musa's rescue from
the water.*

The Birth of Musa/Moses

*There it is written
that Allah had already promised the mother
 that Allah would take care of her son
and bring him back to her,
and that Allah would make him one of
    Allah's messengers.
That is what happened.*

Musa/Moses in the Royal Palace
(Exodus 2:11–15; Surah 28:14–21)

Moses grew up in the palace of Pharaoh.
When he had grown up, he went to see
   the Israelites,
both books tell us.
He could see for himself
how they bent under the slavery.
He also saw an Egyptian beating a Hebrew
—one of Moses' own people.
Moses got so angry
that he killed the Egyptian.

He quickly hid his body in the sand.

Another day he again went out to his people.
Then he saw two of them
fighting, and he asked the one who
   was wrong,
"Why do you beat your brother?"
But he became afraid when the man replied,
"Who made you our ruler and judge?
Are you going to kill me
just as you killed that Egyptian?"
"What shall I do?" Moses thought.
"People have found out what I have done."
Indeed, it became dangerous for him;
for when Pharaoh heard what had happened,
he sought to kill Moses.

*There came a man, running,
from the farthest end of the city,
the Qur'an tells us. He said,*

57

Unit 4: Musa/Moses

*"O Musa, the king's chiefs are planning
to kill you. So go away,
for my advice is true!" (Surah 28:20).
And Musa did so.
Looking about in fear he ran
and prayed to Allah, "O my Lord!
Save me from these wrong-doing people!"
So he fled into the desert,
towards the land of Madyan.*

Musa/Moses in the Land of Midian
(Exodus 2:16–22; Surah 28:22–28)

So Moses fled to the land of Midian

> *—that's Madyan in the Qur'an;*
> *in that book it is written that Musa said,*
> *"I do hope that my Lord will show me*
> *the smooth and straight path" (Surah 28:22).*

He sat down by a well—both books tell us.
Young women came to the well
to draw water and fill the troughs
for their father's sheep and goats.
They were daughters of Jethro,
the priest of Midian, the Bible tells us.
But soon, shepherds came
to draw water for their own animals;
they drove Jethro's daughters away.
Moses again noticed an injustice,
and he stepped in and helped the women
water their animals.
Their father was surprised to see
his daughters coming back so early.
They told him about the young man by
   the well.
"Why did you leave him out there?" he asked.
"Invite him to come and eat with us."
Then one of the daughters went back to
   the well.

> *She was feeling shy, the Qur'an says;*
> *for it was not normal*
> *for a woman to speak to an unknown man.*

Unit 4: Musa/Moses

> *"My father invites you to his house,*
> *so that he may reward you*
> *for having watered our flocks for us," she said.*
> *So he came to her father*
> *and told his whole story.*
> *Then her father said, "Don't fear;*
> *you have escaped from unjust people."*
> *One of the daughters said,*
> *"O my father, employ this man;*
> *truly, the best man for you to employ*
> *is the man who is strong and trusty."*
> *The father had a plan. He said to Musa,*
> *"I intend to wed one of my daughters to you,*
> *if you serve me for eight years.*
> *And if you complete ten years,*
> *it will be a grace for you;*
> *but I intend not to place you under strain.*
> *If Allah wills, you will find me one of*
>   *the righteous."*

Moses agreed to live there,
taking care of Jethro's sheep and goats.

He married Zipporah and they had a son;
his name was Gershom.

Musa/Moses Called by God
(Exodus 2:23—4:17; Surah 28:29–35)

So Moses served his father-in-law.
But in Egypt the Israelites were
   still groaning
under the slavery.
Both books tell us about it.

Sometimes, the people cried out for help.
Their cry went up to God;
God heard it—the Bible says—
and God remembered the covenant
with Abraham, Isaac, and Jacob.

Then it happened that one day,
near the mountain Horeb

—*Mount Tur in the Qur'an*—

Moses saw
a bush was on fire
but it was not burning up.

*The Qur'an says that it happened
when Musa had fulfilled his obligation
and was traveling with his family.*

When Moses wanted to come closer
to see that strange event,
a voice called to him from the bush,
"Moses! Moses!"

Moses said, "Here I am."
"Don't come any closer," the voice called,
"because you are standing on holy ground.

Unit 4: Musa/Moses

> *"I am Allah; there is no god but Me, so worship*
> *Me and keep up the prayer so you*
> *remember Me" (Surah 20:13–14).*

I am the God of your ancestors,
the God of Abraham, Isaac, and Jacob.
I have seen how cruelly my people are being treated
in Egypt, and I have heard them cry out
to be rescued from their slave drivers.
I know all about their sufferings.
I have come down to rescue them from the Egyptians
and to bring them out of Egypt to a spacious land,
one which is rich and fertile,
with plenty of milk and honey.
Now I am sending you to the king of Egypt,
so that you can lead my people out of his country."
Then Moses became frightened and he said to God,
"I am nobody. How can I go to the king
and bring the Israelites out of Egypt?"
But God answered, "I will be with you;
and when you bring the people out of Egypt,
you will worship me on this mountain.
That will be the proof that I have sent you."
But Moses was not yet reassured.
He said to God,
"When I go to the Israelites and say to them,
'The God of your ancestors sent me to you,'
they will ask me, 'What is God's name?'
So what can I tell them?"
Then God said to Moses,
"I AM WHO I AM.
This is my name forever.
So this is what you must say to them,
'I AM has sent me to you,
the Lord of your ancestors,
the God of Abraham, Isaac, and Jacob.' "
Then Moses answered the Lord,
"But suppose the Israelites do not believe me
and will not listen to what I say.
What shall I do if they say
that you did not appear to me?"

> In both books the answer of the Lord is this:
> "What are you holding?"
> "A staff," Moses answered.
> The Lord said, "Throw it on the ground."

> When Moses threw it down,
> it turned into a snake, and Moses ran away
>   from it.
> But God said, "Put out your hand
> and pick it up by the tail."
> Moses did so and the snake became
>   a staff again.
> The Lord spoke to Moses again,
> "Put your hand inside your robe."
> Moses obeyed; and when he took his hand out,
> it was covered with white spots, like snow.
> Then the Lord said,
> "Put your hand inside your robe again."
> He did so and when he took it out this time,
> it was healthy again.

"These are two miracles for the Israelites;
if they are not convinced by the first miracle,
then this second one will convince them
that the God of their ancestors appeared to you."

> *Musa spoke to Allah,*
> *"O my Lord, I have slain a man among them,*
> *and I fear lest they slay me.*
> *And my brother Harun is a much better speaker*
> *than I am: so send him with me as a helper,*
> *to confirm and strengthen me"*
> *(Surah 28:33–34).*

In the Bible, Harun is Aaron.

> *In the Qur'an he is called a prophet of Allah*
> *like Musa (Surah 19:53; Exodus 4:1).*
> *Then Allah promised Musa*
> *that Allah would send Harun with him*
>   *to Fir'awn.*

But God also reminded Moses,
"Who gives speech to mortals?
Who makes them mute or deaf,
seeing or blind?
Is it not I, the LORD? (Exodus 4:11) Now, go!
 I will help you to speak
And I will tell you what to say."
But when Moses still answered,
"No, Lord, please send someone else,"

Unit 4: Musa/Moses

God really became angry.
Yet God told Moses that Aaron, Moses' brother,
was already on the way to Moses.
And God promised Moses
that God would also be there.
"Take your staff with you," God added,
"for with this staff you will perform miracles."

Musa/Moses and Harun/Aaron Go to Fir'awn/Pharaoh
(Exodus 5—11; Surahs 26:16–51; 40:28–34; 7:133–135)

So Moses and Aaron

    —Musa and Harun in the Qur'an—

went together to Pharaoh

    —Fir'awn in the Qur'an.

The Qur'an and the Bible tell us about it.
The two men said to Pharaoh,
"We are the messengers of the Lord.

The LORD, the God of Israel says,
'Let my people go, so that they may celebrate a festival
to me in the desert' " (Exodus 5:1b).
But Pharaoh said, "Who is the LORD,
to whom I should listen and let Israel go?
I don't know the LORD,
and I will not let Israel go."

    The Qur'an gives Musa's answer,
    "Allah is He, the Lord and Cherisher
    of the heavens and the earth, and all between;
    and the Lord of the East and the West,
    and all between! So send with us
    the children of Israel."
    But Fir'awn said, "I don't know the Lord
    and I will not let Israel go."

Unit 4: Musa/Moses

> He got angry and said to Musa, "Did we
>   not cherish
> you as a child among us,
> and did you not stay in our midst
> many years of your life?
> And you did something you know you did

—he killed the Egyptian, didn't he?—

> and you are an ungrateful man!"
> Musa replied, "I did it then,
> when I was in error.
> So I fled from you, when I feared you.
> But my Lord has since invested me
> with judgment and wisdom
> and the Lord appointed me
> as one of the Lord's messengers.
> And is this the favor with which you approach me,
> that you have enslaved the children of Israel?"
> Fir'awn said to the Israelites around him,
> "Your messenger is a veritable madman!"
> And to Musa he said,
> "If you take any god other than me,
> I will certainly put you in prison!"
> But Musa said,
> "Even if I showed you something
>   clearly convincing?"
> Fir'awn replied, "Show it then,
> if you tell the truth!"
> (Surah 26:23–31).

Then Moses and Aaron performed
the first miracles, with the snow-white spots
   on their hands,
and with the staff turning into a snake.
Then Pharaoh called for his wise men and for
magicians, sorcerers; and they did the same
with their robes and staffs.
But the staff of Moses and Aaron
swallowed all the other staffs.

> Then the sorcerers fell down, the Qur'an says,
> and they prostrated in adoration, saying,
> "We believe in the Lord of the Worlds,
> the Lord of Musa and Harun."
> But Fir'awn said, "Believe you in the Lord

Musa/Moses and Harun/Aaron Go to Fir'awn/Pharaoh

before I give you permission?
I am your master!"
And he thought of a heavy punishment for them.
But they said, "No matter!
For us, we shall but return to our Lord!
Our only desire is that the Lord will forgive us
our faults" (Surah 26:46–51).
Then the Qur'an tells about a man,
from among the people of Fir'awn,
who had concealed his faith.
He said, "Will you slay a man
because he says, 'My Lord is Allah,'
when he has indeed come to you
with clear signs from your Lord?
And if he be a liar, on him is his lie.
But if he is telling the truth,
Then there will fall on you something of
the calamity of which he warns you:
truly, Allah guides not one
who transgresses and lies!
O my people, yours is the dominion this day,
but who will save us from the punishment of Allah,
should it befall us?"
Fir'awn said,
"I but point out to you that which I see;
nor do I guide you but on the path of the right!"
Then the man who believed said,
"O my people! Truly I do fear
for something like the day of disaster,
something like the people of Nuh;
then you will have nobody to protect you.
Allah does not allow injustice to his servants."
And he reminded them of Yusef,
who, although he was not an Egyptian, came with
clear signs from Allah
and saved the nation from a famine
(Surah 40:28–34).
"O my people! This life of the present
is nothing but temporary enjoyment:
it is the hereafter that is the home
that will last.
One who works evil will receive only evil,
but one who works a righteous deed
and is a believer—whether man or woman—
such will enter the Garden of Bliss"
(Surah 40:39–40).

But Pharaoh didn't want to listen.
Both books mention the plagues that hit
Pharaoh and his people:
locusts, boils on their skin,
the Nile water changing into blood,
frogs, gnats, flies,
hailstones, thick darkness, and a cattle plague.
Only the Israelites were saved by the Lord.

*In the Qur'an an infestation of lice is named
as one of the plagues (Surah 7:133).*

Pharaoh was arrogant until a plague hit
   the Egyptians.
Then he said again and again to Moses,
"Pray for us to your God
because of what God ordered you to do.
If you can stop the plague,
we shall truly believe your words
and send away the Israelites with you."
But each time a plague was removed
   from them,
Pharaoh broke his word.
Then the tenth plague came over them.
In the Bible it is written that God told Moses
that before Pharaoh would let him go,
the last plague would be this:
every firstborn son in Egypt would die
and the firstborn of all the cattle as well.
Moses gave this message to Pharaoh.
Thereafter, he left Pharaoh in great anger.
In both books it is written
that the Lord said to Moses
to leave that very night,
because they would be persecuted.

That night, the Israelites ate in Egypt
for the last time.
Moses had ordered them to bake their bread
in a hurry, without preparing leavened dough.
They also had to kill a lamb or a young goat
and smear its blood on the doorposts
as a sign that Israelites were living in this house.
And when the meat of that animal was prepared
and they were dressed for the journey,
they ate in a hurry.

That very night, God's angel killed
all firstborn Egyptian sons
and the firstborn of all the cattle,
as Moses had warned the king before (Exodus 4:23).
But all houses with blood on the doorposts
were passed by the angel
and the dwellers in those houses were saved.
Then Pharaoh—whose firstborn son also died—
called Moses and Aaron by night and said,
"Be ready to go away, out of the midst of my people,
you and all Israelites as well.
Go and celebrate your Lord as you have said.
Take also your flocks and herds, but go!"
And his last words to Moses were,
"Also pray for a blessing on me."
The Egyptians urged the people to hurry
and leave the country; they said,
"We will all be dead if you don't leave."
And when the Israelites asked the Egyptians
for gold and silver jewelry and for clothing,
they gave them what they asked for.
The people filled their baking pans
with unleavened dough, wrapped them in clothing,
and carried them on their shoulders,
so they could bake on their way.
Then a very large number of Israelites set out on foot:
six hundred thousand men, not counting women
   and children.
A large number of other people also went with them
and many sheep, goats, and cattle.
They left Egypt four hundred thirty years
after Jacob and his family had arrived there,
the Bible says.
They also took the body of Joseph with them,
as was promised to him before his death.
(This night of departure has become
the Passover festival for all Israelites,
to honor the Lord.
And the month of the Passover festival
has become for them the first month of the Hebrew year.
Passover is still celebrated in the houses
with a meal of a slaughtered lamb or goat
and unleavened bread
on the evening of the fourteenth day
of that first month.)

Musa/Moses with the Israelites through the Red Sea
(Exodus 13:17—15:21; Surahs 20:77; 26:52; 26:60–66; 44:23–24)

God

—Allah in the Qur'an—

led Moses with the Israelites
in the direction of the Red Sea.

During the day the Lord went in front of them
 in a pillar of cloud, to show them the way,
and during the night the Lord went in front of them
in a pillar of fire, to give them light,
so that they could travel by day and by night.

But soon after Israel's departure from Egypt
Pharaoh regretted
having let the Israelites go.
Both books tell us so.
One day at sunrise the Israelites saw
they were being pursued by Pharaoh
with all the horses, chariots, and drivers,
and they were terrified and
cried out to the Lord for help.

"We are sure to be overtaken!"
was their cry in the Qur'an.
But Musa said, "By no means!
My Lord is with me!
Soon the Lord will guide me!"
(Surah 26:61–62.)

Unit 4: Musa/Moses

In the Bible, Moses' words are,
"Don't be afraid!
Stand firm, and see the deliverance
that the LORD will accomplish for you today;
for the Egyptians whom you see today
you shall never see again.
The LORD will fight for you,
and you have only to keep still" (Exodus 14:13–14).

> So they moved forward to the Red Sea.
> Then the Lord said to Moses,
> "Lift up your staff, stretch it out over the sea;
> strike the water and it will divide,
> and the Israelites will be able
> to walk through the sea on dry ground."

And Moses did so; he held his hand over the sea,
and the Lord drove the sea back
with a strong east wind. It blew all night
and turned the sea into dry land.
The pillar of fire that had been in front of the Israelites
moved and went behind them;
and the pillar of cloud also moved
until it was between the Egyptians and the Israelites.
The cloud made it dark for the Egyptians,
but the pillar of fire gave light to the people of Israel.
So the Israelites went through the sea
with walls of water on both sides.
The Egyptians pursued them
and went after them into the sea
with all their horses, chariots, and drivers.
Just before dawn, the Lord looked down
at the Egyptians.
The Lord made the wheels of their chariots get stuck,
so that they moved with great difficulty.
The Egyptians cried out,
"The Lord is fighting for the Israelites
against us!"

> *In the Qur'an it is written,*
> *"We (Allah) revealed to Moses: 'Strike the sea*
>   *with your staff!' It parted—each side like*
> *a mighty mountain—and we brought the others*
>   *to that place. We saved Musa and all*
> *his companions and drowned the rest"*
> *(Surah 26:63–66).*

Musa/Moses with the Israelites through the Red Sea

Then the Lord again said to Moses,
"Hold out your hand over the sea,
and the water will come back
over the Egyptians and their chariots and drivers."
Moses did so and at daybreak
the water returned to its normal level.
It covered the chariots, the drivers
and all of the Egyptian army; not one of them was left.
On that day the Lord saved the people of Israel
from the Egyptians.
Then Moses and the Israelites
sang a song to the Lord,
"I will sing to the LORD,
for God has triumphed gloriously;
horse and rider God has thrown into the sea.
The LORD is my strength and my might,
and God has become my salvation;
this is my God, and I will praise the LORD,
my father's God, and I will exalt God"
(Exodus 15:1b–2).
And the prophet Miriam, sister of Moses and Aaron,
took her tambourine,
and all the women followed her,
playing tambourines and dancing.
Miriam sang for them,
"Sing to the LORD; for God has triumphed gloriously;
horse and rider God has thrown into the sea"
(Exodus 15:21).

Unit 5
The Desert Journey

Beginning of the Desert Journey
(Exodus 15:22—17; Surahs 2:57; 7:138–141; 20:80–82)

After praising the Lord,
Moses led the people away from the Red Sea
into the desert of Shur.

> *The Qur'an says that they came upon a people*
> *devoted entirely to some idols they had;*
> *in Arabic such devotion is called "shirk."*
> *The Israelites said,*
> *"O Musa, fashion for us a god*
> *like the gods they have."*
> *But Musa said,*
> *"You don't know what you are asking for.*
> *The cult these people are in*
> *is bound to destruction,*
> *and they worship in vain.*
> *Shall I seek for you*
> *a god other than Allah, when it is Allah*
> *who has endowed you with gifts above*
> *   other nations?*
> *Allah rescued you from Fir'awn's people!"*
> *(Surah 7:138–141).*

For three days they walked through the desert,
without finding water.
Then they came to a place called Marah,
but the water there was so bitter that they could not
    drink it.
They complained to Moses and asked
"What are we going to drink?"
Moses prayed earnestly to the Lord,
and God showed him a piece of wood,

which Moses was to throw into the water;
then the water became fit to drink.
God also promised them
that God always would help them
if they listened to God, and
did what God considered right,
and kept God's commands.
The Lord led them to a place called Elim,
with twelve springs and seventy palm trees;
there they camped by the water.
After Elim, the Israelites went up
to the desert of Sin, between Elim and Sinai.
There their food ran out and they
complained to Moses and Aaron,
"Better the Lord had killed us in Egypt;
there we could eat meat and other food
as much as we wanted."
But Moses said,
"When you complain against us,
you are really complaining against the Lord."
Then the Lord came in a cloud
and spoke to Moses,
"I have heard the complaints of the Israelites.
Tell them that at twilight they will have meat to eat,
and in the morning they will have all the bread
   they want.
Then they will know that I, the Lord, am their God."

> In the evening, a large flock of quails flew in,
> enough to cover the camp,
> and in the morning there was dew all round
>   the camp.
> When the dew evaporated, there
>   was something
> thin and flaky on the surface of the desert.
> It was as delicate as frost.

When the Israelites saw it they didn't know
 what it was and they asked each other,
"What is it?"
Moses said to them, "This is the food
that the Lord has given you to eat.
The Lord has commanded that each of you
is to gather as much of it as you need,
two liters for each member of your household.
No one is to keep any of it for tomorrow."

But some of them did not listen to Moses
and saved part of it. The next morning
it was full of worms and smelled rotten,
and Moses was angry with them.
Every morning, each one could gather
as much as was needed to bake and to boil.
And when the sun grew hot,
what was left on the ground melted.
On the sixth day, they gathered twice as much food,
four liters for each person,
as Moses said to the leaders,
"The Lord has commanded that
tomorrow is a holy day of rest,
dedicated to the Lord.
So bake today what you want to bake
and boil what you want to boil.
Whatever is left should be put aside
and kept for tomorrow."
So the people did this
and the food did not spoil or get worms in it.
On the seventh day, some of the people
went out to gather food, but they did not find any.
Then the Lord said to Moses,
"How much longer will your people refuse to obey
    my commands?
Remember that I, the Lord,
have given you a day of rest
and that is why on the sixth day
I will always give you enough food for two days."
The people of Israel called the food manna.
It was like a small white seed
and tasted like biscuits made with honey.
Moses said,
"The Lord has commanded us to save some manna,
to be kept for our descendants,
so that they can see the food
which the Lord gave us to eat in the desert
when the Lord brought us out of Egypt."

> Everywhere they walked
> along the way to the Promised Land,
> they found the manna in the morning.
> But not the water;
> again they complained to Moses about
>   the water,
> before they listened to the Lord.

The Bible and Qur'an tell us so.
However, God persisted in care for the people.
The Lord said to Moses,
"Take some of the leaders of Israel with you,
and go ahead of the people.
Take along the staff with which you struck
 the Nile.
I will stand before you on a rock at
 Mount Sinai.
Strike the rock, and water will come
 out of it
for the people to drink."
And so it happened.
As Moses did it in the presence of the
 leaders of Israel,
they could see for themselves, and tell
 the others,
that it was the Lord who gave the water.

In the Desert of Sinai
(Exodus 19)

Three months after the Israelites had left Egypt,
they came to the desert of Sinai.
There they set up camp at the foot of Mount Sinai.

> *In Arabic the name is Mount Tur;*
> *this is the holy place where Musa*
> *saw the bush on fire that did not burn up*
> *(Surah 28:29–35).*

Moses went up the mountain to meet with God.
There the Lord told Moses about God's plans for
　God's people,
the Israelites, if they obeyed God
and kept God's covenant.
So Moses went down and called
the leaders of the people together
and told them everything that the Lord had
　commanded him.
The leaders passed it on to all the people.
Then the Israelites answered together,
"We will do everything that the Lord has said";
and Moses reported this to the Lord.
The Lord said,
"Tell the people to spend today and tomorrow
purifying themselves for worship.
They must wash their clothes and be ready
the day after tomorrow. On that day I will come down
on Mount Sinai, where all the people can see me.
Tell them not to go up the mountain
or even get near it."
So it happened.

Unit 5: The Desert Journey

> *In the Qur'an it is written that*
> *before he went up*
> *Musa charged his brother Harun,*
> *"Act for me among my people.*
> *Do right, and follow not the way of those*
> *who do mischief" (Surah 7:142).*

Then Moses went up to God
and Aaron stayed with the people.

> There is much written in both books
> about what happened high up on
>   the mountain
> and down in the desert.

God and Idol
(Exodus 20—33; Surahs 7:142–145, 148–156; 20:86–94)

On the mountain of Sinai much
  was discussed
between God and Moses.
God gave him the Ten Commandments,
written on two stone tablets,
and a great number of other laws and rules.

God also told Moses how to build an altar
for the sacrifices of the Israelites.
The sacrifices had to be offered by
Aaron and his sons.
Aaron was to be anointed high priest
and his sons priests;
special clothes had to be made for them,
exactly conforming to what God told Moses.
A tent of the Lord's Presence (called a tabernacle) also
  had to be made,
and a covenant box (called the Ark of the Covenant)
  with a lid,
to be put in the tent with all the other furniture.
God gave exact instructions for
how everything had to be made.
Therefore it took a long time
before Moses came down again
—forty days.

> *In the Qur'an is written*
> *that Allah appointed for Musa thirty nights,*
> *and completed the period with ten more*
> *(Surah 7:142).*

The Israelites didn't understand
why their leader stayed away so long.

Unit 5: The Desert Journey

Then they said to Aaron,
"We do not know what has happened
to this man Moses, who led us out of Egypt;
so make us a god to lead us."
And on Aaron's instruction all people took off
their gold earrings and brought them to him.
Aaron took the earrings, melted them,
poured the gold into a mold,
 and made a gold bull.
Then the people said,
"Israel, this is our god, who led us out of Egypt!"

> *"Shirk" is the Arabic word for such idolatry.*
> *In the Qur'an, Allah's words are written:*
> *"Did they not know that an idol*
> *neither can speak to them nor show the way?"*
> *(Surah 20:89).*

Aaron also built an altar, and he announced,
"Tomorrow there will be a festival
to honor the Lord."
Early the next morning they brought some animals
to burn as sacrifices,
and others to eat as fellowship offerings.
The people sat down, eating, drinking, and feasting.
But there were also people who did not participate.
Those were the Levites, men of the tribe of Levi,
one of Jacob's sons.

> Then Moses came down from the mountain.
> In his hands he held the two stone tablets
> with the Ten Commandments of God.
> God had already told him on the mountain
> what was happening down in the desert.
> "Go back down at once," God said,
> "because your people, whom you led
>   out of Egypt,
> have sinned and rejected me.
> They have already left the way
> that I commanded them to follow;
> they have made a bull out of melted gold
> and have worshiped it and offered sacrifices
>   to it.
> They are saying that this is their god,
> who led them out of Egypt."

God and Idol

> In anger God also said
> that God was going to destroy them.

"Then I will make you and your descendants
into a great nation," the Lord said.
But Moses pleaded with the Lord, saying,
"Lord, why should you be so angry with your people,
whom you rescued from Egypt with great might
   and power?
Why should the Egyptians be able to say
that you led your people out of Egypt,
planning to kill them in the mountains
and destroy them completely?
Stop being angry; change your mind
and do not bring this disaster on your people.
Remember your servants Abraham, Isaac, and Jacob."
Now that Moses himself heard the noise
of the shouting people,
and saw the bull, and the people dancing,
he too became furious;
he threw the two stone tablets of the
   Ten Commandments
 and shattered them to pieces
at the foot of the mountain.

> *The Qur'an tells us that Musa,*
> *angry and grieved, said to the people,*
> *"You have done evil*
> *in my absence: did you make haste*
> *to bring on the judgment of your Lord?"*
> *Moses seized his brother by his head*
> *and dragged him to him. Harun said,*
> *"Son of my mother! The people pressed me*
> *and nearly killed me! You know how they are.*
> *Make not the enemies to rejoice over*
>   *my misfortune,*
> *nor count me among the people of sin"*
> *(Surah 7:150).*

The Bible also mentions such words.
Moses said to Aaron,
"What did these people do to you,
that you have made them commit such a terrible sin?"
Aaron answered: "Don't be angry with me;
you know how determined these people are to do evil.
They said to me: 'We don't know what has happened

Unit 5: The Desert Journey

to this man Moses, who brought us out of Egypt;
so make us a god to lead us.'
I asked them to bring me their gold ornaments,
and those who had any took them off
and gave them to me. I threw the ornaments
into the fire and out came this bull!"
Moses saw that Aaron had let the people
get out of control and make fools of themselves
in front of their enemies.

> *The Qur'an says that Musa prayed to the Lord,*
> *"O my Lord! Forgive me and my brother!*
> *Admit us to your mercy!*
> *For you are the most merciful of those who show*
> *mercy" (Surah 7:151).*

Moses took the bull which they had made,
melted it, ground it into fine powder,
and mixed it with water,
and he made all idolaters drink it.
Moses stood at the gate of the camp and shouted,
"Everyone who is on the Lord's side come over here!"
So all the Levites gathered round him.
He ordered them on behalf of the Lord
to kill the idolaters.
On that day many Israelites died.
The next day, Moses said to the people,
"You have committed a terrible sin.
But now I will again go up the mountain to the Lord;
perhaps I can obtain forgiveness for your sin."
Moses then returned to the Lord and said,
"These people have committed a terrible sin.
They have made a god out of gold and worshiped it.
Please forgive them their sin; but if not,
then remove my name from the book
in which you have written the names of your people."
The Lord answered,
"It is those who have sinned against me
whose names I will remove from my book.
Now go, lead the people to the place I told you about.
Remember that my angel will guide you;
if I were to go with you even for a moment,
I would completely destroy you.
Now take off your jewelry,
and I will decide what to do with you."
Moses repeated God's words for the people.

God and Idol

When they heard these words, Israel mourned;
and they did not wear jewelry any longer.
Some distance away from the camp,
Moses had put up the sacred tent.
Anyone who wanted to consult the Lord
could go into it.
Whenever Moses went there,
the people stood at the door of their tents
to watch him until he entered.
After Moses had gone in,
the pillar of cloud would come down
and stay at the door of the tent,
and the Lord would speak to Moses from the cloud.
As soon as the people would see the pillar of cloud
at the door of the tent, they would bow down,
everyone at the door of God's tent.
Then the Lord spoke with Moses face to face,
just as a person speaks with a friend.
One time Moses went to God's presence for himself.
He said to the Lord,
"It is true that you have told me
to lead these people to that land,
but you did not tell me whom you would send
   with me.
You have said that you know me well
and are pleased with me.
Now if you are, tell me your plans,
so that I may serve you and continue to please you.
Remember also that you have chosen
this nation to be your own."
Then the Lord said,
"Shall I go with you to put you at ease?"
Moses replied, "If you don't go with us,
Don't make us leave this place.
How will anyone know
that you are pleased with your people and with me,
if you do not go with us?
Your presence with us will distinguish us
from any other people on earth."
Then the Lord said,
"I will do just as you have asked,
because I know you very well
and I am pleased with you."

The Commandments
(Exodus 20:1–17; 25—30; 34—35; Surah 7:145)

Another time Moses went up the mountain
to meet with God. God said to him,
"Cut two stone tablets like the first ones,
and I will write on them the words
that were on the first tablets, which you broke.
Be ready tomorrow morning, and come up Mount Sinai
to meet me at the top."
Moses did so.
The Lord came down in a cloud.
Moses quickly bowed down to the ground
and worshiped. He said,
"Lord, if you really are pleased with me,
I ask you to go with us.
Forgive our evil and our sin,
and accept us as your own people."
Then God made a covenant with Israel through Moses.
The Lord promised to do great things in their presence,
such as had never been done anywhere on earth
among any of the nations. All the people would see
the great things God could do.
Moses, on behalf of the people,
had also given promises to the Lord
that God's laws would be obeyed;
that no treaties would be made
with the people of other countries;
that they would not worship any other god,
as the Lord tolerated no rivals;
that they would keep the Festival
of Unleavened Bread in the month of Abib,
because it was in that month that they left Egypt;
that every firstborn son and firstborn domestic animal
　belonged to God
as a sacrifice; the firstborn son

would then be bought back with a sacrificial animal,
as no one was to appear before God
without an offering.
Also the best of the first harvest
had to be brought to the house of the Lord.
After six days of working,
the seventh day had to be a day of rest,
even during plowing time or harvest.
And three times a year all believers had to come
to worship the Lord, the God of Israel.
And God said,
"Write these words down,
because it is on the basis of these words
that I am making a covenant with you
and with Israel."
And God wrote the Ten Commandments
on the two new stone tablets.
And God gave more guidelines to Moses.
So Moses stayed another forty days and nights
with the Lord.
But now the Israelites did wait for him
till he came down with both stone tablets.
Aaron and all the people looked at Moses
and saw that his face was shining,
and they were afraid to go near him;
but Moses did not know it and he called them.
Aaron and all the leaders of the community
went to him, and Moses spoke to them.
The leaders, obliged to set a good example,
heard from Moses the Ten Commandments,
given by the Lord on the two stone tablets from the
    Mount of Sinai:
"Worship no god but me.
Do not make for yourselves images.
Do not bow down to any idol or worship it.
Do not use my name for evil purposes.
Observe the Sabbath and keep it holy.
Respect your father and your mother.
Do not commit murder.
Do not commit adultery. (This commandment is also
    found in the Qur'an.)
Do not steal.
Do not accuse anyone falsely.
Do not desire anything of another."
And the Great Commandment of God

The Commandments

was given by Moses with these words,
"Hear, O Israel:
The LORD is our God, the LORD alone.
You shall love the LORD your God
with all your heart,
and with all your soul,
and with all your might.
Keep these words that I am commanding you
today in your heart.
Recite them to your children
And talk about them when you are at home and when
   you are away,
when you lie down and when you rise.
Bind them as a sign on your hand,
fix them as an emblem on your forehead,
and write them on the doorposts of your house
and on your gates" (Deuteronomy 6:4–9).

> *Each of the Ten Commandments*
> *is also mentioned in the Qur'an.*
> *"We (Allah) inscribed everything for him in the*
> *Tablets, which taught and explained everything,*
> *saying, 'Hold onto them firmly and urge your*
> *people to hold fast to their excellent teachings.'*
> *Here is guidance and mercy for those who do*
> *wrong, then repent afterwards and truly*
> *believe" (Surah 7:145,154).*
> *About parents the Qur'an says*
> *"that you be kind to parents.*
> *Whether one or both of them attain*
> *old age in your life, say,*
> *'My Lord! Bestow on them your mercy*
> *even as they cherished me in childhood"*
> *(Surah 17:23–24).*
> *Allah also ordered care for the poor,*
> *for the needy, for orphans,*
> *for the suppressed people,*
> *for those who are in your debt*
> *and also for the indigent*
> *(Surahs 9:60; 76:8–9; 90:15–17).*
> *And as in the Bible,*
> *in the Qur'an the Great Commandment is this:*
> *"The Lord is Allah, the One!" (Surah 112:1).*

Unit 5: The Desert Journey

After all these commandments and the instructions
on how to worship the Lord,
the Israelites built a new tent of the Lord's presence
and made precious furniture for it,
just as the Lord had commanded.
They also made the covenant box
and the clothes for the high priest and the priests.
Meanwhile, Aaron and his sons learned all the
    prescripts for worshiping
that the Lord had given to Moses.
The Israelites worked for a long time.
When everything was ready,
they dedicated the tent of the Lord's presence
and all its equipment
by anointing it with the sacred oil.
Aaron and his sons were dressed and anointed
as high priest and priests.
And Aaron blessed the people of Israel
with the words given by God,
"May the LORD bless you and keep you;
the LORD make his face to shine upon you
and be gracious to you;
the LORD lift up his countenance upon you,
and give you peace" (Numbers 6:24–26).
And the Lord said,
"If the priests in this way pronounce my name
as a blessing upon the people of Israel,
I will bless them" (Numbers 6:22–27).
After these dedications,
the Israelites carefully packed up everything
and started on their journey
out of the Sinai desert,
led by Moses and Aaron.

In the Desert of Paran
(Exodus 25—26; Numbers 10—11; 13—14; Surahs 2:57, 61; 5:20–26)

When Moses and Aaron left Sinai with the people,
they traveled for three days.
They took the tent of the Lord's presence (also called
  the Tabernacle) with them,
woven of fine linen and wool and embroidered in colors.
Its frame was made of wood and covered with gold.
The tent was covered with several pieces of cloth
made of goat's hair, ram's skin, and fine leather,
to protect it against the weather.
The Lord's covenant box (also called the Ark of
  the Covenant)
was being carried ahead to find the next place to camp.
The box was made of wood covered with pure gold;
and golden carrying rings were fitted
for its four acacia wooden legs.
The lid of the box was made of pure gold,
with two winged creatures of hammered gold on it,
forming one piece with the lid.
Two wings were spread upward and the other
two covered the lid.
The two stone tablets of the Ten Commandments
were carried in the box
as a reminder of the covenant God would keep
if the people continued listening to the Lord.

> *The Qur'an also mentions the box*
>   *of the covenant;*
> *in it lay assurance of safety from the Lord*
> *and the relics left by the family of Musa*
> *and the family of Harun as a symbol*
> *for those who have faith (Surah 2:248).*

Unit 5: The Desert Journey

So the Lord's covenant box went ahead;
the two poles through the four golden rings
were carried on the shoulders of four strong men.
The Lord's cloud went on above the box,
showing the way to the next place.
After three days, they arrived in the desert of Paran,
where Hagar and Ishmael had lived long ago.
There the cloud stayed.

> The people set up their camp
> and also found manna every morning.
> But they began murmuring again.
> The complaints came first from people
> who were not Israelites, but foreigners,
> traveling with them since Egypt.
> But later everybody murmured; both books
> > tell us so.

> > *In the Qur'an it is written that the people said,*
> > *"O Musa! We cannot stand having only one*
> > > *kind of food.*
> > *So beg your Lord on our behalf to produce for us*
> > *what the earth grows: potherbs and cucumbers,*
> > *its garlic, lentils, and onions."*
> > *He said, "Will you change the better for the worse?*
> > *Go down to any town and you shall find what*
> > > *you want!" (Surah 2:61).*

The Bible also mentions people's complaints,
"If only we could have some meat!
In Egypt we used to eat all the fish we wanted,
and it cost us nothing.
And remember the cucumbers, the watermelons,
the leeks, the onions, and the garlic we had!
But now our strength is gone.
There is nothing at all to eat
—nothing but this manna day after day!"
Moses heard all the people complaining
as they stood at the entrance of their tents.
He was distressed and said to God,
"Why have you given me the responsibility
for all these people? Where could I get
enough meat for them all?
I can't be responsible for all the people
myself; it's too much for me!
If you are going to treat me like this,

take pity on me and kill me."
Then the Lord said,
"Gather seventy respected men
who are recognized as leaders of the people,
bring them to me at the tent of my presence.
I will take some of the spirit I have given you
and give it to them. Then they can help you
to bear the responsibility for these people,
and you will not have it to bear alone.
Now tell the people: 'Purify yourselves for tomorrow;
you will have meat to eat, not just for one or two days,
or five, or ten, or even twenty days,
but for a whole month,
until it comes out of your ears,
until you are sick of it; this will happen,
because you have complained to the Lord
that you should never have left Egypt.' "
And so it happened.
Seventy men were assembled
and God blessed them with the Spirit,
so that they could help Moses with his work.
And God sent a wind that brought quails from the sea.
They settled on the camp and all round it
for many miles in every direction.
So that day and night and the next day
the people worked catching quails.
While the meat was yet between their teeth,
before it was consumed, the anger of the Lord
was kindled against the people,
and God smote them with a very great plague.
That place was named Kibroth-hattaavah,
which means "graves of craving,"
because there were buried the people who
had craved meat (Numbers 11:31–34).
From there the people moved
through the desert of Paran, to Haseroth,
where they made camp.
Now they were already near to the Promised Land.
The Lord said to Moses, "Choose one of the leaders
from each of the twelve tribes,
and send them as spies to explore the land of Canaan,
which I am giving to the Israelites."
Moses obeyed and chose the twelve men
and told them the message of the Lord.
He said,
"Go into the southern part of the land of Canaan

Unit 5: The Desert Journey

and then on into the hill country.
Find out what kind of country it is,
how many people live there, and how strong they are.
Find out whether the land is good or bad
and whether the people live in open towns
or in fortified cities.
Find out whether the soil is fertile
and whether the land is wooded.
And be sure to bring back
some of the fruits that grow there."
It was the season when grapes were beginning
　to ripen.
The men did what Moses had said
and after forty days they returned to
Moses, Aaron, and the whole community of Israel.
They reported what they had seen
and showed them the fruit they had brought:
one bunch of grapes, so heavy
that it took two men to carry it
on a pole between them. They also
brought back some pomegranates and figs.
And they told about the fertile land,
and about the powerful people
and the large and fortified cities
where giants lived.
Yet Caleb, one of the two men who trusted God,
said, "We should attack now and take the land;
we are strong enough to conquer it,
if we have trust in God."
But the other ten men said,
"No, we are not strong enough to attack them;
the people there are more powerful than we are."
And they made the people afraid.

The Qur'an tells us that Musa said,
"O my people! Remember God's favor for you,
when Allah gave you what Allah had not given
to any other people.
Enter the holy land which Allah has assigned
*　to you."*
But they said, "O Musa!
In this land are a people of exceeding strength:
We will not enter it
until they leave it.
If they leave, then we shall enter.
You go, and your Lord,

> *and you two fight, while we sit here"*
> *(Surah 5:20–24).*

All night long the people cried out in distress.
They complained against Moses and Aaron, and said,
"It would have better to die in Egypt
or even here in the wilderness!
Why is the Lord taking us into that land?
We will be killed in battle,
and our wives and children will be captured.
Wouldn't it be better to go back to Egypt?"
So they said to one another,
"Let's choose a leader and go back to Egypt!"
Then Moses and Aaron bowed down to the ground
in front of all the people.
And Joshua and Caleb, the two men who trusted in God,
tore their clothes in sorrow and said to the people,
"The land we explored is an excellent land.
If the Lord is pleased with us, God will take us there
and give us that rich and fertile land.
Do not rebel against the Lord
and don't be afraid of the people who live there.
We will conquer them easily.
The Lord is with us and has defeated the gods
who protected them; so don't be afraid."
The whole community was threatening
to stone them to death; but suddenly the people saw
the dazzling light of the Lord's presence
appear over the tent.
The Lord said to Moses,
"How much longer will these people reject me?
How much longer will they refuse to trust in me,
even though I have performed so many miracles
among them?
I will send an epidemic and destroy them,
but I will make you the father of a nation
that is larger and more powerful than they are!"
But Moses said to the Lord,
"You brought these people out of Egypt by
   your power.
When the Egyptians hear what you have done
to your people, they will tell the people
who live in this land.
These people have already heard that you, Lord,
are with us, that you are plainly seen
when your cloud stops over us,

and that you go before us in a pillar of cloud by day
and a pillar of fire by night.
Now if you kill all your people,
the nations who have heard of your fame will say
that you killed your people in the wilderness
because You were not able to bring them
into the land you promised to give them."
And Moses continued,
"So now, Lord, I pray, show us your power
and do what you promised when you said,
'I, the Lord, am not easily angered,
and I show great love and faithfulness
and I forgive sin and rebellion,
although I will not fail to punish.'
So now, Lord, according to the greatness
of your unchanging love, forgive, I pray,
the sin of these people, just as you
have forgiven them ever since they left Egypt."
After this prayer from Moses the Lord answered,
"I will forgive them, as you have asked.
But I promise that as surely as I live,
and as surely as my presence fills the earth,
none of these people, except Caleb and Joshua,
will live to enter that land,
which I promised to their ancestors."

> *Musa said, "Lord, I have authority over no one except myself and my brother; judge the two of us and those disobedient people." Allah said to him, "This land is forbidden to them. For forty years they will wander the earth aimlessly. Do not grieve over the ones who disobey"*
> *(Surah 5:25–26).*

And the Lord continued,
"Now give the people my answer,
'You said that your children would be captured,
but I will bring them into the land that you rejected,
    and it will be their home. You will die
here in the wilderness.
Your children will wander in the wilderness
for forty years, suffering for your unfaithfulness,
until the last one of you dies.
Turn back tomorrow and go into the wilderness
in the direction of the Red Sea.
You will know what it means to have me against you!'"

When the Israelites heard what the Lord had said,
they mourned bitterly.
But early the next morning they started out
to invade the hill country, saying,
"Now we are ready to go to the place
which the Lord told us about.
We admit that we have sinned."
But Moses said,
"Why are you disobeying the Lord?
You will not succeed. Don't go!
The Lord is not with you,
and your enemies will defeat you."
Yet they dared to go up into the hill country.
But they were attacked, defeated, and pursued.

Back into the Desert
(Numbers 20; Deuteronomy 31—34; Surahs 19:51; 33:69)

So the Israelites could not do anything else
but go back into the desert.
This became a difficult time,
a time of worry and sorrow,
and a time of quarrel and disobedience.
Even Moses lost his patience.
Once again there was no water
and the people gathered around Moses and Aaron,
complaining and accusing them both
of having brought them out of Egypt to die.
Then Moses and Aaron moved away from the people
and stood at the entrance of the tent.
They bowed down with their faces to the ground,
and the dazzling light of the Lord's presence
appeared to them.
The Lord said to Moses,
"Take the staff that is in front
of the covenant box, and then you and Aaron
assemble the whole community.
There, in front of them all,
speak to that rock over there,
and water will gush out of it.
In this way you will bring water
out of the rock for the people,
for them and their animals to drink."
Moses went and got the staff,
as the Lord had commanded.
He and Aaron assembled the whole community
in front of the rock, and Moses said,
"Listen, you rebels! Do we have to get water
out of this rock for you?"
Then Moses raised the staff
and struck the rock twice with it,

and a great stream of water gushed out,
and all the people and animals drank.
But the Lord reprimanded Moses and Aaron.
The Lord said, "Because you did not have enough faith
to acknowledge my holy power
before the people of Israel,
you will not lead them into the land
that I promised to give them."
And so it happened.
Moses was called by God
to climb up the Mount of Hor,
together with Aaron and Aaron's son Eleazar.
So they went up in the sight of the whole community.
There, Moses removed Aaron's priestly robes
and put them on Eleazar.
Then, Aaron died on the top of the mountain,
and Moses and Eleazar came back down.
Later the Lord called Moses and said to him,
"You haven't much longer to live.
Call Joshua and bring him to the tent,
so that I may give him his instructions."
Moses went to the tent, together with Joshua.
Then the Lord appeared to them in a pillar of cloud.
And the Lord said to Moses,
"Place your hands on his head.
Make him stand in front of Eleazar the priest
and the whole community. And before them all
proclaim him as your successor."
Moses did so.
Then the Lord said to Joshua,
 "Be confident and determined.
You will lead the people of Israel
into the land that I promised them,
and I will be with you" (Numbers 27).
And to Moses, the Lord said,
"You shall write a song and teach it
to the people of Israel.
For I will take them into this rich and fertile land,
as I promised their ancestors.
They will have all the food they want,
and they will live comfortably.
However, a time will come when they turn away
    from me
and worship other gods. They will reject me
and break the covenant that I made with them.

But this song will still be sung,
and it will stand as evidence against them."
That same day, Moses wrote down the song
and taught it to the people of Israel.
He recited the entire song
while all the people of Israel listened.
Then he sang it for the Israelites,
together with Joshua.
So the people learned the song.
And for their children it is written in the Bible
(Deuteronomy 32).
When Moses had finished
writing God's law on a scroll,
he said to the Levitical priests,
"Take this book of God's law
and place it beside the covenant box,
so that it will remain there
as a witness against God's people.
Make sure you obey all these commands
that I have given you today.
Repeat them to your children,
so that they may faithfully obey all God's teachings.
These teachings are not empty words;
they are your very life.
Obey them and you will live long
in that land across the Jordan
that you are about to occupy."
Then, Moses gave a speech
to these younger people,
telling them all that had happened
in all those years of traveling through the desert.
For they did not have that experience
because many of them were born in the desert.
Their parents, who were slaves in Egypt,
died in the meantime.
Now these young men and women were the
   new generation
that was allowed to enter into the Promised Land.
Finally, Moses blessed his people.
He gave a blessing to each of the
twelve tribes of the Israelites.
Thereafter, he climbed up Mount Nebo, alone.
And God showed him the whole land
where the twelve tribes were going to live,
each in its own place.

Then the Lord took the life of Moses
and his grave was never found.
It is written in the Bible that
there has never been a prophet in Israel like Moses:
the Lord spoke with him face to face.
No other prophet has ever done miracles and wonders
like those that the Lord sent Moses
to perform against the king of Egypt.
No other prophet has been able to do
the great and terrifying things
that Moses did in the sight of all Israel.

> *And in the Qur'an this message to Muhammad
>   is written:*
> *"Also mention in the book the story of Musa;*
> *for he was specially chosen.*
> *He was a messenger and a prophet*
> *(Surah 19:51).*
> *You all who believe!*
> *Be not like those who hurt Musa.*
> *Allah cleared him of the lies they had uttered.*
> *And he was honorable in Allah's sight"*
> *(Surah 33:69).*

Since Moses had put his hands
on Joshua's head to bless him,
Joshua was filled with wisdom.
The people of Israel obeyed him
and kept the commands
that the Lord had given them through Moses;
so it is written in the Bible.

Unit 6
Guides, Judges, and Kings

Guides and Judges
(Judges 2:1—3:4; 1 Samuel 2:11—7:1; Surah 2:246–248)

It was more difficult than expected
for the people of Israel to live without
such leaders as Moses or Joshua.
As long as there were elders who had seen
the great miracles of God, things were all right.
But after that whole generation had died,
the Israelites did what was right in their own minds.
The stories of Israel were no longer told much,
so the children often did not hear
what the Lord had done for Israel.
The less they heard from their own people,
the more they saw of the people around them.
They saw the idols and how people worshiped them,
and they often decided to participate in this worship.
The Lord had warned them against this evil many times
and had forbidden it.
So the Lord became furious with Israel
and let raiders attack and rob them.
The Lord allowed their enemies all around to
    overpower them,
and the Israelites could no longer protect themselves.
They groaned under their suffering and they cried;
then the Lord had mercy on them.
God gave Israel leaders
to deliver them from their enemies
and to guide them on the right way to God.
In the Bible, such a person is called a "judge,"
as he or she also judged cases of conflicts.
But whenever a judged died, the Israelites
behaved even worse than before.
This happened several times.
Finally God sent Samuel.
In the Bible he is known as a famous judge and prophet,

> *and in the Qur'an he is called*
> *a prophet of the Israelites,*
> *but his name is not mentioned (Surah 2:246).*

Samuel was a leader of the Israelites for a long time.
He also reprimanded Eli,
priest of the house of the Lord in Shiloh.
Eli didn't watch his two priest sons
and didn't take care of the house of the Lord
and of the box of the covenant that
held the Ten Commandments.

> *The Qur'an also speaks of*
> *the Ark of the Covenant as a sign of security*
> *from the Lord and says that in it are the relics*
> *left by the family of Musa and Harun.*
> *It will be carried by angels (Surah 2:248).*

Eli's two sons did bad things in God's holy place.
Once they even fetched the Lord's covenant box
to take it to their army.
For the Israelites fought against the Philistines
and they were not able to conquer them.
Therefore they had said, "Let's go and bring
the Lord's covenant box from Shiloh,
to go with us and save us from our enemies."
But they were wrong, as God did not go with the Ark.
God had already told Samuel
that God was very angry because of
all the evil in God's holy place,
and that a punishment would come.
And so it happened that in the battle
with the Philistines, the Israelites lost.
Eli's sons were killed
and the Ark was taken by the enemies.
When someone came to Shiloh to tell the news
to Eli, Eli fell backward,
broke his neck, and died.
So all three died because of
the evil they had done toward God.
And the Israelites were very frightened.
God also let it be known to the Philistines
that they were not allowed to take the Ark.
Wherever they put the Ark, something bad happened.
First, they took it into the temple of their god Dagon,
in Ashdod, and set it up beside his statue.

Early next morning, the people of Ashdod saw
that the statue of Dagon had fallen
face down to the ground,
in front of the Ark of Israel's God.
So they lifted it up and put it back in its place.
Early the following morning, they saw
that the statue had again fallen down
in front of the covenant box.
This time, its head and arms were broken off
and were lying in the doorway;
only the body was left.
The Lord punished the people of Ashdod severely,
by causing them to have tumors.
Then they said, "The God of Israel is punishing us
and our god Dagon."
They took the Ark to the city of Gath,
but there again God punished the people with tumors
and with a plague of mice.
So these people sent the box to Ekron,
another Philistine city,
but when it arrived there, the people cried out,
"They have brought the covenant box
of the God of Israel here, in order to kill us all!"
Then they sent for all Philistine kings
and said, "Send the covenant box of Israel
back to its own place, so that it won't kill us
and our families."
Tumors also developed in Ekron
and the people cried out to their gods for help.
So God's Ark came back to Israel again
after seven months. It was placed on a wagon
pulled by two cows that were to leave their calves behind.
For the people had said,
"If the cows don't return to their young,
but go straight in the direction of Israel,
then this is a sign for us:
that the box indeed has to go back to that country,
and that it is the God of Israel
who has sent this terrible disaster on us.
In that case, we also have to offer something to the Lord
for the wrong we did by taking the Ark with us."
So they made five gold models of mice
and five gold tumors, as a symbol and a memory
of the plagues of Israel's God;
they were put in a box beside the covenant box.
The people of Beth-shemesh were harvesting wheat

in the valley, when suddenly they looked up
and saw the covenant box.
The wagon was pulled by two mooing cows.
The five Philistine kings followed them
as far as the border of Beth-shemesh.
That day was a day of celebration in Beth-shemesh.
The people chopped up the wooden wagon,
killed the cows and offered them
as a burnt sacrifice to the Lord.
The five Philistine kings watched them do this
and then went back to Ekron that same day.
But when the people of Beth-shemesh became
curious and looked into the covenant box,
the Lord killed seventy of them.
The people got very frightened and they said,
"Who can stand before the Lord, this holy God?
Where can we send the Ark to get the Lord away
    from here?"
They sent messengers to the people of Kirjath-jearim,
in their neighborhood, to tell them
that the Philistines had returned the Lord's covenant box,
and they asked them to come down and fetch the box,
So the people of Kiriath-jearim fetched the box
and took it to the house of a man named Abinadab,
who lived on a hill.
They consecrated his son Eleazar to be
in charge of it.

Israel's First King—Talut/Saul
(1 Samuel 8—17; Surah 2:246–251)

When Samuel grew old, he made his sons,
Joel and Abijah, judges in Israel.
But they did not follow their father's example
and they did not decide cases honestly.
Then all leaders of Israel met together
and went to Samuel. They said to him,
"Look, you are getting old
and your sons don't follow your example.
Appoint a king to rule over us,
so that we will have a king as other countries have."
Samuel was displeased with their request for a king;
so he prayed to the Lord; and the Lord said,
"Listen to everything the people say to you.
You are not the one they have rejected;
it is me who they have rejected as their king.
So then, listen to them, but give them strict warnings
and explain how their king will treat them."
So Samuel did; he told them what a king would claim
from their crops, their sons, their possessions;
but the people persisted in asking for a king
who would lead them to war to fight their battles.

The Qur'an also mentions this request
  of the Israelites,
and it says that later,
when their king commanded them to fight,
they turned back (Surah 2:246).

That king was Saul from the tribe
  of Benjamin.

In the Qur'an, Saul is called Talut.

Samuel anointed Saul as king over
the people of Israel.
"You will rule these people," he said,
"and protect them from all their enemies."

> *The prophet said to them, "Allah has appointed*
> *Talut to be your king." But they said,*
> *"How can he be king over us when we have*
> *a greater right to rule than he?*
> *He does not even have great wealth."*
> *He said, "Allah has chosen him over you, and*
> *has given him great knowledge and stature"*
> *(Surah 2:247).*

When Saul turned to leave Samuel, God gave Saul
a new nature, and suddenly the spirit of God
took control over him.
So Saul could be a good king for his people
as long as he listened to the Lord.
But a time came when Saul no longer
did so. He felt strong and went his own way.
Then the Lord withdrew the spirit from Saul.
And God sent Samuel to Saul to reprimand him
in the name of God, and to say that, because he
 disobeyed God,
he could no longer be a king.
Samuel was sent by God to Bethlehem,
to a man called Jesse, a father with seven sons.
The youngest one was David; he was a shepherd.

> *In the Qur'an, his name is Dawud.*

He was anointed king by Samuel.
David first remained at home
to take care of his father's sheep.
His brothers were commanded by king Saul
to become soldiers in his army.

> They had to fight against the Philistines,
> and especially against the Philistine
> called Goliath
>
> *—Jalut in the Qur'an.*

> He is mentioned in both books.
> Goliath was a giant and everyone was
> afraid of him.

Once, David went to his brothers,
on behalf of his father, to take them food
and to ask them how they were getting on.
When he was talking to his brothers,
the giant Goliath came forward,
challenging the Israelites and cursing their God.
David perceived how afraid they were
and he said, "Who is this heathen Philistine
to defy the army of the living God?"
These words of David were told to Saul,
and Saul sent for David. David said to Saul,
"No one should be afraid of this Philistine!
I take care of my father's sheep.
Whenever a lion or a bear carries off a lamb,
I go after it, attack it, and rescue the lamb.
And if a lion or bear turns on me,
I grab it by the throat and beat it to death.
The Lord has saved me from lions and bears;
God will also save me from this Philistine."
"All right," Saul answered; and he gave his own
armor to David to wear.
David tried to walk, but he couldn't.
So he took it all off.
He took his shepherd's staff and then picked up
five smooth stones from the stream
and put them in his bag. With his sling ready,
he went out to meet Goliath.
The Philistine came closer,
and when he got a good look at David,
he called down curses from his god on David.
But David said,
"You are coming against me with sword, spear,
and javelin, but I come against you in the name of
the Lord Almighty, the God of the Israelite army,
which you have defied.
This very day the Lord
will be victorious in the battle
and will put all of you in our power.
Then the whole world will know that Israel has a God."

> *When they met Goliath and his warriors, they*
> *said, "Our Lord, pour patience on us; make us*

> *stand firm and help us against the disbelievers."*
> *So, with Allah's permission, they defeated him*
> *(Surah 2:250–251).*

And David put his hand into his bag, took out a stone,
and slung it at Goliath. It hit him on the forehead
and broke his skull, and Goliath fell face downward
on the ground. David ran to him, stood over him,
took Goliath's sword out of his sheath,
and cut off his head.

>So he killed him.

When the Philistines saw that their hero was dead,
they ran away. The men of Israel shouted
and ran after them, pursuing them all the way to Gath
and to the gates of Ekron.
David stayed in the charge of Saul
and he became the friend of Saul's son Jonathan.
Later, Saul separated himself from God.
In a war against the Philistines
he and two sons died; one of them was Jonathan.

>Then David became king in Saul's place.

Dawud/David–King of Israel
(2 Samuel 1—2:6; 11—12; Surah 38:21—25)

When David heard that Israel had lost the war,
and that Saul and two of his sons had died,
he fasted and mourned. He also wrote and sang a
    lament song;
and he ordered it to be taught
to the people of Judah.
One of the verses was to his friend Jonathan:
"I am distressed for you, my brother Jonathan;
greatly beloved were you to me" (2 Samuel 1:26).
David wrote and sang many songs,
accompanying himself on the harp.

> *Allah knows best about everyone in*
> *the heavens and the earth.*
> *"We gave some prophets more than others.*
> *We gave Dawud a book (of psalms)" (Surah 17:55).*

He had done this for Saul in the past,
when Saul was suffering from an evil spirit,
and Saul would calm down.
Many of David's songs are included in the Bible,
    as psalms.
There are morning psalms and evening psalms,
psalms of joy and psalms of sadness,
psalms of trust and psalms of fear,
prayers for help and protection,
and psalms of thanksgiving to the Lord
for saving from distress.
David also wrote pilgrim songs.

> *Allah also gave psalms to Dawud,*
> *the Qur'an tells us (Surah 4:163).*
> *Allah graced Dawud with his favor.*

> He said, "You mountains, echo Allah's
> praises together with him,
> and you birds also" (Surah 34:10).

David also wrote a psalm of repentance;
he sang and prayed that psalm,
after the prophet Nathan had come to him.

> In the Qur'an it is written that two brothers
> who came to him asking him to 'judge between
>   us fairly—do not be unjust—and guide
> us to the right path.
> My brother has ninety-nine sheep and I just
>   the one,
> and he said, 'Let me take charge of her,' and he
> overpowered me with his words."
> Dawud said, 'He has done you wrong by
> demanding to add your one to the flock."
> Then Dawud realized that Allah had been
>   testing him
> and he realized his wrong in not listening
> to both sides before making a judgment.
> He asked his Lord for forgiveness,
> fell down on his knees and repented.
> Allah forgave him, and said,
> "Dawud, We have given you mastery over
>   the land.
> Judge fairly between people" (Surah 38:22–26).

Nathan told David a story
about a rich man who possessed many sheep
and a poor man who had only one sheep.
That poor man was ordered to give his sheep
to the rich man, because the rich man had visitors
and didn't like to slaughter one of his own sheep
for the meal.
The Bible tells that when David heard the story,
He got very angry with that rich man.
He said to the prophet Nathan
that the man must be killed.
But Nathan said to David,
"You are that man. For you, who have enough,
have taken Bathsheba, the only wife of Uriah,
your officer in the army,
and you had Uriah put in a dangerous place
to have him killed."

David was very frightened by Nathan's words
and by his own order to kill the rich man
of the story.
He said, "I have sinned against the Lord."
Nathan replied,
"The Lord forgives you; you will not die,
but the newborn son of you and your new wife
    will die."
And that happened.
Then David sang a psalm of repentance (Psalm 51).

> Their next son lived; that was Solomon.

In the Qur'an he is called Sulaiman
(Surah 38:30).

> David was a good king of Israel for a
> long time.

He was crowned in Hebron as king of Judah for
    seven years,
and then in Jerusalem as king of the whole nation
    of Israel
for thirty-three years.

In the Qur'an Allah says he taught
Dawud how to soften iron and
make chain mail coats to protect
his men in their wars (Surah 34:10; 21:80).

In that time, he brought the Ark of the Covenant
to Jerusalem with great celebration.
Dancing and offering sacrifices, David went ahead
    of the Ark.
In Jerusalem, this covenant box was placed in a tent
until the temple of the Lord was built.
It was David's desire to have it built himself.
But the Lord told him through the prophet Nathan
that he was not the one to build the temple.
One of his sons would become king
and he would build God's temple.
And so it happened.

> When David died, his son Solomon
> became Israel's king.

King Sulaiman/Solomon
(1 Kings 2—3; 6; 10—11; Surah 27:20–44)

Solomon became the king after David.
One night, after Solomon was anointed king,
the Lord appeared to him in a dream
and asked him, "What would you like me to give
 to you?"
Then Solomon replied,
"O Lord, you have let me succeed my father as king,
even though I am very young. So give me the wisdom
I need to rule your people with justice
and to know the difference between good and evil."
The Lord was pleased that Solomon asked for this,
and said to him,
"Because you have asked for wisdom to rule justly,
instead of long life for yourself, or riches,
I will do what you have asked.

> "I will give you more wisdom and
> understanding
> than anyone has ever had before or will
> ever have again;

"and I will also give you what you have not asked for:
wealth, and honor, and a long life,
if you obey me and keep my laws
 and commandments."
And so it happened that kings all over the world
heard of Solomon's wisdom and sent people to listen
 to him.

> Also the queen of Sheba
>
> —*Saba, in the Qur'an*—

Unit 6: Guides, Judges, and Kings

came to visit him.

> *In the Qur'an, it is written that Sulaiman*
> *was told about her. He sent her a letter*
> *of invitation, for her and all her officials,*
> *in the name of Allah, Most Gracious,*
>   *Most Merciful,*
> *to come to the king*
> *in submission of the true religion.*
> *Sulaiman wrote it in this way, as he had heard*
> *that it was her custom to worship the sun.*

The queen was amazed
at how great Solomon's wisdom was
in his questions and answers.

> In the Qur'an and the Bible, several
>   examples
> of the great wisdom of this king are given
> (1 Kings 3:16–28; 10:1–13; Surah 27:15–44).

From the fourth to the eleventh year of Solomon's reign,
Solomon worked on building the temple.
It became a beautiful temple,
covered with gold outside and inside.
Finally, Solomon dedicated the temple to the Lord
when they celebrated the Festival of Shelters.
The king summoned all the leaders of the tribes
to come to Jerusalem.
When all the leaders had gathered,
the priests lifted the covenant box,
carried it into the temple, and put it in the Most
    Holy Place.
Then the priests moved the tent of the Lord's presence,
and all its relics from the past, to the temple.
When the priests were leaving the temple,
it was suddenly filled with a cloud
shining with the dazzling light of the Lord's presence.
Then Solomon went and stood in front of the altar,
where he raised his arms and prayed,
"Lord, God of Israel, there is no god like you
in heaven above or on earth below!
You keep your covenant with your people.
You have kept the promises you made
to my father David;
today every word has been fulfilled.

And now, Lord God of Israel, from this time forth
let everything come true that you
promised to my father, David, your servant."
And the Lord replied,
"I have heard your prayer.
I consecrate this temple that you have built
as the place where I shall be worshiped forever.
I will watch over it and protect it for all time.
If you will serve me in honesty and integrity,
as your father David did, and if you obey my laws
and do everything I have commanded you,
I will keep the promise I made to your father David
when I told him that Israel would always be ruled
by his descendants.
But if you or your descendants stop following me,
if you disobey the laws and commandments I have
   given you
and worship other gods, then I will remove
my people Israel from the land that I have given them
and I will also abandon this temple, which I
   have consecrated
as the place where I am to be worshiped."
For a long time Solomon was in prayer, kneeling down
on the ground with uplifted hands.
Then the king stood up and turned to face the people,
and he gave them the Lord's blessing,
"May you, God's people, always be faithful
to the Lord our God, obeying all God's laws
and commandments, as you do today."
Then King Solomon, and all the people who were
   gathered there,
offered sacrifices to the Lord
during the seven days of the Festival of Shelters.
On the eighth day, Solomon sent the people home.
They all praised their king and went home happy,
because of all the blessings that the Lord had given
(1 Kings 6—8).
Solomon had many wives from other countries.
Those women brought their own gods with them.
Solomon built places of worship
where all his foreign wives could offer
sacrifices to their own gods (1 Kings 11:1–13).
By the time he was old they had led him
into the worship of their gods,
although the Lord had appeared to him twice
and had commanded him not to worship foreign gods.

Unit 6: Guides, Judges, and Kings

The Lord was very angry with Solomon
and said to him,
"Because you have deliberately broken
your covenant with me and disobeyed
   my commandments,
and not set yourself an example for your son,
he will not be able to reign over the whole country.
I promise that I will take the kingdom away from you
and give it to one of your officials.
I will leave your son only one tribe,
for the sake of my servant David
and for the sake of Jerusalem,
the city I have made my own."
And so it happened.
Only the lands of Judah and Benjamin were
for Solomon's son Rehoboam.

> *The Qur'an says, "Some of those who had*
> *received Scripture before, threw the*
> *Book of God over their shoulders*
> *as if they had no knowledge, and*
> *followed what the evil ones had*
> *fabricated about the kingdom of Soloman instead.*
> *Not that Soloman himself was a disbeliever.*
> *It was the evil ones who were disbelievers;*
> *they taught people witchcraft"*
> *(Surah 2:101–102).*

Kings and Prophets
(1 Kings 18; Surahs 37:123–132; 6:86)

After Solomon's death nearly all the successive kings
continued worshiping idols.
As a result, the people of Israel followed
and they left the Lord.
However, God still sent prophets to the people.
The first of these was Elijah.

> *In the Qur'an, his name is Ilyas.*
> *Ilyas came to the Israelites, the Qur'an says,*
> *and he asked them, "Will you not fear Allah?*
> *Will you call upon Ba'al and forsake*
> *the best of creators, the Lord and Cherisher*
> *and the Lord and Cherisher of your fathers of old?"*
> *But they rejected him (Surah 37:123–132).*

This prophet is also written about in the Bible.
On Mount Carmel he demonstrated to the Israelites
that only God is the Lord, and not Ba'al.
It had not rained for three years
because the people worshiped Ba'al.
The Ba'al priests prayed to Ba'al for hours and hours,
imploring Ba'al to allow it to rain,
but nothing happened.
Then Elijah sacrificed and prayed to the Lord,
asking God for rain.
And the Lord immediately sent down fire,
and it burnt up the sacrifice.
When the people saw this, they threw themselves
on the ground and exclaimed,
"The Lord is God, the Lord is God!"
That day, heavy rain began to fall.

Unit 6: Guides, Judges, and Kings

After Elijah was gone, Elisha became
a prophet of God.

In the Qur'an his name is Alisa'.

He took the prophet's robe that was left behind
when Elijah was taken up to heaven.
Elisha had the same power to do things
as his master Elijah had done.
As a prophet he took action against Israel's enemies
when they came with their armies.
And the enemies stood in awe of Israel's Lord
(2 Kings 6—8; Surah 36:48).
In this way, there were many prophets
who set the right example to the kings and the people.

In the Qur'an, Job is also called a prophet;
there, his name is Aiyub; he cried to the Lord,
"Satan has afflicted me with distress
  and suffering!"
And Allah said,
"Truly, we found him full of patience
  and constancy.
How excellent is this servant; ever did he turn
  to us!
And we gave him back his people and doubled
  their number,
as a grace from us, and for commemoration,
for all who have understanding" (Job, passim;
  Surah 38:41–44).
In the Qur'an too, Yunus (Jonah) is mentioned
as an example to Muhammad.
Yunus had to give Allah's message
to the sinning people of Nineveh;
Yunus fled away by boat, but was thrown
  overboard
because he was found guilty of causing the
  heavy storm;
and he was swallowed by a big fish
and prayed for forgiveness to the Lord
in the belly of the fish;
and the Lord heard Yunus and made the fish
spare Yunus (Surah 37:139–148).

The Bible also tells this story;
here the prophet's name is Jonah.

Kings and Prophets

> After the fish spewed Jonah up
> he went to Nineveh to warn the people,
> and they converted to the Lord.
> So the Lord did not punish that city
> (Surahs 21:87; 68:48–50; 37:139–148).

Jonah was angry, and he regretted warning them.
Then the Lord spoke sternly to Jonah.
The Lord pointed out to him that the great number
    of human beings
and all the children living in that city—
more than a hundred and twenty thousand people
as well as many animals—were all God's creatures.
A prophet of the Lord should not neglect them,
should he? (Jonah, passim).

> The Lord sent other prophets to
>   the Israelites,
> but their names are not mentioned in the
>   Qur'an (Surah 40:78).
> Those are the prophets who told the people
> the messages from God.
> Those prophets' words are included
>   in the Bible
> as messages from God.

Exile
(2 Kings 17:1–6; 25:1–12; Ezra, passim; Nehemiah passim; Daniel 11:1–14; Surah 17:4–8)

> So again and again God sent prophets
> to the people of Israel, to remind them of
> the covenant that they had made with
>   the Lord,
> a covenant of faithfulness and obedience.

For God loved Israel as a father loves his child
   (Hosea 11:1–4),
and God saw the covenant with Israel as a
covenant between a bridegroom and a bride
(Isaiah 62:5; Jeremiah 2:2).
But in spite of this, the people again and again
turned away from God.
Finally, God's patience ran out.

> The Lord sent enemies who occupied the
>   people's land,
> destroyed their cities,

and took the Israelites
as exiles to their countries;
first the ten tribes (Israel) to Assyria
and later the two tribes (Judah) to Babylon.
But the Lord did not forget the people.
The prophet Jeremiah wrote a letter
to the exiles in Babylon.
On behalf of God, he told them
to build in the new place houses for themselves
and to plant gardens to be able to eat their own crops;
to get their children married
and so begin a new life there.
God also told them, through Jeremiah,

Unit 6: Guides, Judges, and Kings

"Only when Babylon's seventy years are completed
    will I visit you,
and I will fulfill to you my promise
and bring you back to this place.
For surely I know the plans I have for you, says
    the LORD,
plans for your welfare and not for harm,
to give you a future with hope.
Then when you call upon me and come and pray
    to me,
I will hear you.
When you search for me, you will find me;
If you seek me with all your heart,
I will let you find me, says the LORD,
and I will restore your fortunes
and gather you from all the nations
and all the places where I
have driven you, says the LORD,
and I will bring you back to the place from which
I sent you into exile" (Jeremiah 29:10a–14).
That is mentioned in Jeremiah's letter,
sent to the exiles in Babylon.
So it happened:
After seventy years, Babylon was occupied by
    the Persians.
And God gave a good spirit
to the king of Persia, Cyrus,
so that he sent the Israelites back
to rebuild Jerusalem and the temple (Ezra, passim).
Then many people returned and repaired
the temple and Jerusalem's walls, as well as they could.
Afterward, they opened the temple
to worship the Lord.
When they heard Ezra read the words of the law,
they promised wholeheartedly to keep all that God
    had dictated.
Thereafter, they lived in peace in their own land
for a long time.

> *And We [Allah] gave (clear) warning to the*
> *Children of Israel in the Book that twice*
> *would they spread corruption*
> *on the earth and be arrogant*
> *(and twice would they be punished)!*
> *When the first of the warnings came*

> *to pass We sent against you Our servants given to*
> *terrible warfare: They destroyed your homes;*
> *and it was a warning (completely) fulfilled.*
> *Then did We allow you to defeat them.*
> *Then We gave you increase*
> *in resources and offspring.*
> *When the second of the warnings came to pass,*
> *(We permitted your enemies) to shame you and to*
> *enter your Temple as they had before and to visit*
> *with destruction all that fell into their power.*
> *It may be that your Lord may (yet) show mercy*
> *unto you; but if ye revert (to your sins) We shall*
> *revert (to Our punishments) (Surah 17:4–8).*

Later, the Persians were conquered by the Greeks,
who occupied Israel's land;
and after that, the Greeks surrendered to the Romans.
The land and people of Israel suffered heavily
under all those rulers.

Unit 7
The Births of Jesus/'Isa and John/Yahya

Zakaria/Zechariah and His Wife, Elizabeth
(Luke 1:5–25; Surahs 3:38–41; 19:2–11)

So now it was the Romans who ruled the land
and the people of Israel.
The Romans had other customs and other gods.
But Israel's priests were still in charge of the temple,
and there the people worshiped the Lord.
In the Bible, one of the daily services
in particular is mentioned.
That was the day Zechariah was working
as a priest in the temple.

In the Qur'an, his name is Zakaria.

It was his turn to burn incense on the altar,
so he went into the temple of the Lord,
while the crowd of people outside prayed.
In both books—the Qur'an and the Bible—
   this is written.
While Zechariah was doing his work,
an angel of the Lord appeared to him
on the right side of the altar.
Zechariah was afraid when he saw the angel.
But the angel said to him,
"Don't be afraid, Zechariah, for your prayer
   has been heard.
Your wife Elizabeth will bear you a son,
and you will name him John.

"You will have joy and gladness,
and many will rejoice at his birth,
for he will be great in the sight of the Lord
He must never drink wine or strong drink;

Unit 7: The Births of Jesus/'Isa and John/Yahya

even before his birth he will be filled
with the Holy Spirit.
He will turn many of the people of Israel to the Lord
   their God.
With the spirit and power of Elijah
he will go before him,
to turn the hearts of parents to their children,
and the disobedient
to the wisdom of the righteous,
to make ready a people prepared for the Lord"
(Luke 1:13–17).

> *This son to be born is also mentioned in*
>   *the Qur'an.*
> *There the name of John sounds like "Yahya,"*
> *"a name never given to anyone before,"*
>   *Allah says.*
> *Zakaria could hardly believe it, as he and his wife*
> *had always been childless and were very old now.*
> *But the angel told him, "Your Lord said,*
> *'That is easy for Me:*
> *I created you before, from nothing!' "*
> *Yet Zakaria asked for a sign.*
> *The answer was,*
> *"Your sign shall be that you shall speak to no one*
> *for three days."*

In the Bible, the angel's answer to Zechariah's request
   for a sign is,
"I am Gabriel. I stand in the presence of God,
and I have been sent to speak to you
and to bring you this good news.
But now, because you did not believe my words,
which will be fulfilled in their time,
you will become mute, unable to speak,
until the day these things occur" (Luke 1:19–20).
In the meantime, the people were waiting
   for Zechariah
and they wondered why he was spending such
   a long time in the temple.

> When he came out, he could not speak to them,
> and he made signs to them with his hands.

> *Using signs, he told them*
> *to celebrate Allah's praises*

Zakaria/Zachariah and His Wife, Elizabeth

in the morning and in the evening,
the Qur'an says (Surah 3:41).

So the people understood
that he had seen a vision in the temple.
When his time of service was ended
he went to his home, to his wife Elizabeth.
Some time later Elizabeth became pregnant;
and she did not leave the house for five months.
She said, "This is what the Lord has done for me
when God looked favorably on me and took
away the disgrace I have
endured among my people" (Luke 1:25).

The Child Yahya/John
(Luke 1:57–80; Surah 19:12–15)

When the time came for Elizabeth
to give birth to her baby, she bore a son,
the Bible tells us.
Her neighbors and relatives rejoiced with her.
On the eighth day, they came to circumcise him
and they were going to name him Zechariah
after his father, but his mother said,
"No! His name is to be John."
His father could not yet speak,
but he asked for a writing tablet and wrote,
"His name is John."
And immediately his mouth was opened
and his tongue loosed and, filled with the Holy Spirit,
he thanked God and prophesied,
"Blessed be the Lord God of Israel,
for God has looked favorably on
God's people and redeemed them" (Luke 1:68).
 He said to his newborn son,
"[You] will be called the prophet of the Most High;
for you will go before the Lord to prepare his ways,
to give knowledge of salvation to his people
by the forgiveness of their sins.
By the tender mercy of our God,
the dawn from on high will break upon us,
to give light to those who sit in
darkness and in the shadow of death,
to guide our feet into the way of peace" (Luke 1:76–79).

> *In the Qur'an it is told that Yahya—*
>   *that's John—*
> *later got Allah's message:*
> *"'O Yahya! Take hold of the Book with might.'*

Unit 7: The Births of Jesus/'Isa and John/Yahya

And we gave him wisdom even as a youth,
and pity for all creatures as from us, and purity:
He was devout and kind to his parents,
and he was not overbearing or rebellious.
So peace on him the day that he was born,
  the day that he dies, and the day that he
will be raised up to life again!"
(Surah 19:12–15).

Maryam/Mary

(Luke 1:26–38; Surahs 3:35–37, 42–51; 4:171)

Another message was sent from God
  to the earth.
That message went to Mary.

Maryam is her name in the Qur'an.

Who was she? A girl from Nazareth,
promised in marriage to a man named Joseph,
from the descendants of David, the Bible tells us.

The Qur'an first tells us something about
  her parents.
'Imran is the Arabic name of her father,
and the Qur'an tells that her mother
prayed to Allah,
"O my Lord! I do dedicate to you what is
  in my womb
for your special service.
So accept this of me:
for you hear and know all things."
When she was delivered, she prayed again,
"Behold! I am delivered of a female child.
I have named her Maryam
and I commend her and her offspring
to your protection from Satan,
the rejected one" (Surah 3:36).
When her parents had cared for her for some years,
they took her to the temple
to dedicate her to the Lord,
as they had promised;
and they prayed to the Lord.
The Lord heard the prayer
and graciously accepted her.

Unit 7: The Births of Jesus/'Isa and John/Yahya

She grew in purity and beauty:
to the care of Zakaria she was assigned,
the Qur'an tells us.
(This Zachariah was the priest of the Lord's temple,
he who, together with his wife Elizabeth, prayed
for a son, for a long time.)
In the Qur'an, it is written that every time
Zachariah entered her chamber to see her,
he found her supplied with food.
He said, "O Maryam! Where is this coming from?"
She said, "From Allah, for Allah provides
sustenance to whom He pleases, without measure"
(Surah 3:37).
After growing up in the temple,
Maryam got a message from heaven.
Angels came to her and said,
"O Maryam! Allah has chosen you and
    purified you,
chosen you above the women of all nations.
Allah gives you glad tidings of a Word from Him:
his name will be 'Masih 'Isa' (Messiah Jesus),
    son of Maryam,
held in honor in this world and the hereafter.
He will be in the company of those nearest
    to Allah.
He shall speak to the people
in childhood and in maturity.
And he shall belong to the righteous."
Maryam said, "O my Lord! How shall I have
    a son,
when no man has touched me?"
He said, "Even so; Allah creates what He will;
When the Lord has decreed a matter, the Lord
    but says to it,
'Be!' and it is.
And Allah will teach him the book and Wisdom,
The Tawrat (Torah) and the Injil (Gospel),
and appoint him a messenger
to the children of Israel
with this message,
'I have come to you with a sign from your Lord,
in that I make for you out of clay, as it were,
the figure of a bird, and breathe into it,
and it becomes a bird by Allah's leave;
and I heal those born blind, and the lepers,
and I bring the dead into life by Allah's leave;

*and I know what you eat
and what you store in your houses. Surely,
therein is a sign for you
if you did believe.
And I have come to you to attest the Torah,
which was before me,
and to make lawful to you
part of what was before forbidden to you
with a sign from your Lord.
So fear Allah, and obey me.
It is Allah who is my Lord and your Lord;
then worship Him; this is a way that is straight.' "
This promise given to Maryam was fulfilled later.
The Qur'an names 'Isa,
Allah's Word that He bestowed on Maryam,
"a Spirit proceeding from Him" (Surah 4:171).*

Mary/Maryam
(Luke 1:25–56)

In the Bible it is the angel Gabriel
who is sent to give Mary the good news.
The angel came to her and said,
"Greetings, favored one! The Lord is with you"
(Luke 1:28).
These words affected her and she wondered
what they meant.
The angel said to her,
"Don't be afraid, Mary, for you have found favor
   with God.
And now, you will conceive in your womb and bear
   a son,
and you will name him Jesus.
He will be great, and will be called
the Son of the Most High,
and the Lord God will give him the throne of David.
He will reign over the house of Jacob forever,
and of his kingdom there will be no end"
(Luke 1:30b–33).
Mary said to the angel,
"How shall this be, since I have no husband?"
The angel answered,
"The Holy Spirit will come upon you,
and the power of the Most High will overshadow you;
therefore the child to be born will be holy;
he will be called the Son of God.
And now, your relative Elizabeth in her old age
has also conceived a son;
and this is the sixth month for her
who was said to be barren.
For nothing will be impossible with God."
Then Mary said, "Here am I, the servant of the Lord;
let it be with me according to your word."

Unit 7: The Births of Jesus/'Isa and John/Yahya

Then the angel departed from her (Luke 1:35–38).
Soon afterward Mary hurried off to Elizabeth.
Together they thanked and praised the Lord.
Mary stayed there for about three months,
the Bible tells us.

Unit 8
'Isa/Jesus and Muhammad

The Child 'Isa/Jesus

(Surahs 19:22–33; 23:50; 66:12)

Maryam became pregnant.
She retired to a remote place,
thus it is written in the Qur'an.
In that book, Allah speaks of
"Maryam, the daughter of 'Imran,
who guarded her chastity;
and we breathed into her body of our spirit;
and she testified to the truth of the words
of her Lord and of his revelations,
and was one of the devout servants"
(Surah 66:12).
When the time to give birth was close,
she was in the neighborhood of a
palm tree and a stream, the Qur'an says.
It was quite difficult for her,
but from beneath the palm tree
a voice cried to her not to grieve,
but to eat from the dates
and to drink from the water
and to be refreshed.
"And if you see anyone, say,
'I have vowed a fast to Allah Most Gracious,
and this day will I enter into no talk
with any human being' " (Surah 19:26).
After 'Isa was born, Maryam brought the babe
to her people, carrying him in her arms.
But they said, "O Maryam, truly you
   have brought
a strange thing! O sister of Harun,
your father was not a man of evil,
nor your mother a woman unchaste!"
But she pointed to the babe.

They said, "How can we talk to one
who is a child in the cradle?"
Then the child said,
"I am indeed a servant of Allah;
He has given me revelation and made
   me a prophet;
and He has made me blessed where so ever I be,
and has enjoined on me prayer and charity
as long as I live.
The Lord has made me kind to my mother,
and not overbearing or miserable;
so peace is on me the day that I was born,
the day that I die,
and the day that I shall be raised up
to life again!"
That is the story of 'Isa, the son of Maryam;
it is a statement of truth,
about which they vainly dispute;
so it is written in the Qur'an.

The Child Jesus/'Isa
(Luke 2)

In the Bible, it is written
that Mary's baby was born in Bethlehem,
the city she was traveling to with Joseph.
Joseph had to register himself there,
as he was a descendant of David.
This was ordered by the Roman emperor Augustus.
While they were in Bethlehem,
the time came for the baby to be born.
Mary gave birth to her son,
wrapped him in strips of cloth
and laid him in a manger,
as there was no room for them to stay in the inn.
There were some shepherds in that part of the country
who were spending the night in the fields,
taking care of their flocks.
An angel of the Lord appeared to them,
and the glory of the Lord shone over them.
They were terribly afraid;
but the angel said to them,
"Don't be afraid, for see—I am bringing you
 good news
of great joy for all the people:
to you is born this day in the city of David
a Savior, who is the Messiah, the Lord.
This will be a sign for you:
you will find a child wrapped in bands of cloth
and lying in a manger" (Luke 2:10–12).
Suddenly a great multitude of heaven's angels
appeared with the angel, singing praises to God,
"Glory to God in the highest heaven,
 and on earth peace among those whom he favors!"
(Luke 2:14).

Unit 8: 'Isa/Jesus and Muhammad

When the angels went away from them and
back into heaven, the shepherds said to one another,
"Let's go to Bethlehem and see this thing
that has happened, which the Lord has made
 known us."
So they hurried off and found Mary and Joseph,
and the babe lying in the manger.
When the shepherds saw him, they told them
what the angel had said about this child.
All who heard it were amazed at what the
 shepherds said.
But Mary kept all these things to herself
and thought deeply about them,
the Bible tells us.
And the shepherds returned,
glorifying and praising God
for all they had heard and seen,
just as the angel had told them.
Mary's son was also circumcised on the eighth day
and he received the name of Jesus;
in the language of his country it is Joshua,
which means "God is Savior."

And in the Arabic language of the Qur'an his name is 'Isa.

The child grew and became strong.
He was full of wisdom,
and God's blessings were upon him,
the Bible tells us.
Every year his parents went to Jerusalem
for the Passover festival;
and when Jesus was twelve years old
he accompanied them for the first time.
There, he sat down in the temple with the
 Jewish teachers
day after day, listening to them
and asking questions. All who heard him
were amazed at his intelligent answers.
His parents didn't know that he was there.
After the Passover they looked for him everywhere.
Three days later, they found him in the temple
and were astonished. They did not understand
what he was doing there.
He said to them,
"Why were you searching for me?

Did you not know that I must be in my Father's
    house?" (Luke 2:49).
Jesus grew both in body and in wisdom,
gaining favor with God and with people;
that's what the Bible tells us.

Yahya and 'Isa— John the Baptist and Jesus
(Luke 3:1–22; Matthew 3:1–17; Mark 1:1–13; John 1:19–34; Isaiah 40:3; Surah 19:12)

The Roman emperor Augustus, who had ordered
the whole nation of Israel to register, had died.
After him, the emperor Tiberius ruled over the empire.
In the fifteenth year of his reign,
when Pontius Pilate was governor in Judea
and Herod was his ruler in Galilee,
John, son of Zechariah, received in the desert
   a message from God;
thus it is written in the Bible.
John went throughout the whole territory
of the river Jordan, preaching to the people
that they had to turn away from their sins
and be baptized with the baptism of forgiveness.
"The kingdom of heaven is near!" he called.
People came to him from Jerusalem,
and from the whole province of Judea
and all the land near the river Jordan.
They confessed their sins
and he baptized them in the Jordan.
They called him John the Baptizer.
He was "the voice of one crying out in the wilderness:
'Prepare the way of the Lord,
make his paths straight.
Every valley shall be filled,
and every mountain and hill
shall be made low' " (Luke 3:4b–5a).
The people asked him, "What are we to do, then?"
John answered,
"Whoever has two coats must
share with anyone who has none;
and whoever has food must do likewise" (Luke 3:11).

Some tax collectors came to be baptized,
and they asked him,
"Teacher, what are we to do?"
"Don't collect more than is legal," he told them.
Some soldiers also asked him,
"What about us? What are we to do?"
He said to them,
"Don't take money from anyone by force
and don't accuse anyone falsely. Be content with
 your pay."
But some people wanted to be baptized
just as the children of Abraham were,
without asking what they should do,
John said to them, "Who told you that you
 could escape
the punishment of God? Do those things
that will show that you have turned from your sins!
And don't think you can escape punishment by saying
that Abraham is your ancestor. I tell you
that God can take these stones
and make descendants for Abraham!"
Then John said to the people,
"I baptize you with water;
but one who is more powerful than I is coming:
I am not worthy to untie the thong of his sandals.
He will baptize you with the Holy Spirit and fire"
(Luke 3:16).
At that time, Jesus arrived from Galilee
and came to John at the Jordan to be baptized by him.
But John tried to make him change his mind.
He said, "I need to be baptized by you,
and do you come to me?" (Matthew 3:14).
But Jesus answered him, "Let it be so now;
for it is proper for us in this way
to fulfill all righteousness" (Matthew 3:15).
Then John baptized Jesus.
And when Jesus came up out of the water,
heaven was opened to him and he saw the Spirit of God
coming down like a dove and resting on him.
Then a voice said from heaven,
"This is my Son, the Beloved,
with whom I am well pleased" (Matthew 3:17).
John the Baptist gave the message of God
to many people, with many warnings.

In the Qur'an, it is written that Yahya did what Allah told him to do:
"O Yahya! Take hold of the Book with might" (Surah 19:12).

Herod, the governor of Galilee,
was reprimanded by John because he had married
Herodias, his brother's wife,
and had done many other evil things.
So he put John in prison.
And later he ordered that John be killed,
because his second wife wished it so (Mark 6:14–29).
Jesus said of John
that he was not only a prophet
but more than a prophet (Matthew 11:7–11),
because already in the past
God had said about him through a prophet,
"I am sending my messenger to prepare the way before
 me" (Malachi 3:1).

In the Qur'an Allah says,
"We reward those who do good—
Zakaria, Yahya [John], 'Isa [Jesus] and Eliyah,
every one of them is righteous.
Those are the ones to whom
We gave the Scripture, wisdom, and
 prophethood" (Surah 6:84–85. 89).

'Isa/Jesus and His Disciples
(Matthew 5:1–12; Mark 1:14–20; Luke 7:18–23; Surahs 3:52–53; 5:111; 61:14)

After John had been put in prison, Jesus

> —*in the Qur'an, 'Isa*—

went to Galilee and preached the good news from God.
And, like John, Jesus also said to the people,
"The right time has come and the kingdom of God
  is near!
 Turn away from your sins and believe in the
  good news!"
After that, he told them about the kingdom of God,
the kingdom of heaven that would come on earth,
where the sick are healed,
where poverty and hunger are over,
where evil makes room for love and joy.
And by telling parables, Jesus set examples of
  that kingdom.
Those parables are to be found in the Gospels.

> *The biblical parable of the seed*
> *is also mentioned in the Qur'an (Surah 48:29).*

Jesus was part of that kingdom, saying,
"And this is the will of him who sent me,
that I should lose nothing of all that he has
given me, but raise it up in the last day.
This is indeed the will of my Father,
that all who see the Son and believe in him
may have eternal life; and I will raise them up
on the last day" (John 6:39–40).

> *This last day is also very important in*
> *the Qur'an,*

> *as it is the day of the decision,*
> *where good and bad deeds will become clear*
> *and Allah will judge whether people will be*
> *rewarded or punished (Surah 14:21–24).*

The people heard what Jesus said and asked him,
as they had asked John the Baptist,
"What are we to do? Which commandment
is the most important of all?"
And Jesus said, as Moses said in the past,
"The first is, 'Hear, O Israel: the Lord our God, the
　Lord is one;
you shall love the Lord your God with all your heart,
and with all your soul, and with all your mind,
and with all your strength.'
The second is this, 'You shall love your neighbor
　as yourself.'
There is no other commandment greater
than these" (Mark 12:29–31).

> By Jesus' words, the people saw
> how great was his love for God and for
> 　his neighbors.
> They took to him their relatives and friends
> who were ill: the deaf and blind, the
> 　crippled and lame,
> and those who were possessed by evil spirits.
> Also those inflicted with leprosy came.
> Jesus drove away all people's illnesses,
> and the evil spirits fled from him,
> so that the people who were thus set free
> 　could follow Jesus
> in their right mind.
> He even brought the dead to life again
> and gave them back to those who loved them.

> *This is also mentioned in the Qur'an*
> *(Surah 3:49).*

By working the whole day for the kingdom of God,
Jesus sometimes grew very tired.
Then, he withdrew to a silent place
to rest and pray to God,
to get new strength for the coming day.
He also chose twelve disciples—followers.

'Isa/Jesus and His Disciples

"Follow me," he said, and they followed him
and learned from him how to work for the
   kingdom of God.

> *In the Qur'an they are called helpers*
> *(Surah 61:14).*

Jesus taught the people
what to do for a better life,
for themselves and also for others.
If they did these things, he said, the world would
   resemble the kingdom of God.
Jesus said, "Everything you do
for the hungry, the thirsty, the naked,
the sick, and the foreigner,
you do for me."

> *In the Qur'an it is also written*
> *that alms are for the poor and the needy,*
> *and for those in bondage and in debt*
> *in the cause of Allah, and for the traveler*
> *(Surahs 9:60; 63:10).*
> *The Qur'an says*
> *that you establish a weight with justice*
> *and fall not short in the balance,*
> *that for the love of Allah you feed*
> *the indigent, the orphan and the captive,*
> *saying, "We feed you for the sake of Allah alone:*
>   *no reward do we desire, nor thanks."*
> *This is ordained by Allah;*
> *and Allah knows what is in people's hearts.*
> *Allah is full of knowledge and wisdom*
> *(Surahs 76:8–9; 90:15–17).*

In the Bible, Jesus points out to the people
that everybody is able to do something for others,
as the Lord has given skills to everyone;
in the Bible, those skills are called talents.
Such talents may be skills of your head,
or your heart, or your hands;
sometimes, it may be something you can do with
   your money.

      And the Lord knows very well
      which talents God has given to everyone.
      So, at the end of everyone's life

Unit 8: 'Isa/Jesus and Muhammad

> God will ask each of them what he or she
>   has done
> with the talent God gave them
> (Matthew 25:14–30; Surah 14:51).

Nobody knows when that day of judgment will come,
so everybody has to prepare and always be ready
for the kingdom of heaven.
Jesus told a parable about the kingdom of heaven:
It will be like ten bridesmaids who took their oil lamps
and went out to meet the bridegroom.
But five of them did not take extra oil with them.
The bridegroom was late in coming,
so the girls fell asleep.
It was midnight when the call
to announce that the bridegroom was coming
was heard.
The bridesmaids woke up. The five who had extra oil
filled their lamps, but there was not enough
to share with the others; otherwise all the lamps
might go out and the bridegroom would
come in darkness.
The other five bridesmaids went
to the shop to buy oil for themselves.
But while they were gone, the bridegroom arrived;
he went into the wedding feast with the
bridesmaids present, and the door was closed.
The other five had not welcomed him,
so he didn't know them and they could not come in.
Jesus concluded, "Keep awake therefore, for you
know neither the day nor the hour" (Matthew 25:1–13).

> *Such a warning is also given in the Qur'an;*
> *it is a warning to unbelieving men and women,*
> *that they cannot borrow from the light of others*
> *who are prepared (Surah 57:12–14).*

This message was told in the past
and is still being told today.
Jesus warned the people on behalf of God,
just as John the Baptist had done.
But, as happened in the time of John's warnings,
some people didn't want to listen
to the warnings of Jesus; they got angry and said,
"He behaves like God. The words he says, only God
  can say."

They didn't understand that Jesus spoke
with the authority of God;
and they did not understand that it was with the
   Holy Spirit
that Jesus healed the people
and gave them wholeness.
Some preferred to force Jesus away,
so that they would not need to hear his warnings.
In fact, they wanted to kill him.
Jesus did know that, and again he warned them
(Matthew 21:33–46).
They tried to accuse him of blasphemy, but could not
   prove it.
Then they made up lies and, after several trials,
they succeeded in having Jesus condemned and crucified
at Golgotha, outside Jerusalem.
At noon the whole country was covered
   with darkness, which lasted for three hours.
No light was seen,
no Word of God gave help,
no Spirit of God gave healing and strength.
In that darkness, Jesus cried out,
"My God, my God, why have you forsaken me?"
   and died.
His body was carefully laid in a tomb by good friends
(Matthew 26—27).

> *In the Qur'an it is written that the*
> *Jews did not kill the Masih 'Isa (Messiah Jesus),*
> *nor crucify him, but that Allah took him up to*
> *himself (Surah 4:157–158).*

It is written that two days later,
when the women came to the tomb of Jesus,
an earthquake suddenly began,
and the soldiers who were guarding the tomb
were surprised by a blinding light.
It was an angel, coming from God;
he rolled the stone away and sat on it.
The guards trembled and became like dead men.
Then they fled back to the city
and told the chief priests everything that had happened.
But the angel told the women
that Jesus had been raised from the dead,
and he showed them the place where Jesus had
   been lying.

Then the angel told them to report this message
to the disciples (Matthew 28:1–7).
Jesus himself appeared to the disciples.
"Peace be upon you," he said to them.
And he breathed on them, saying,
"Receive the Holy Spirit!" (John 20:22).

When it was his time to return to God,
Jesus told his disciples
—also called apostles—to go into the world.
The Bible tells us this.
They were to make all people his disciples,
to baptize them and to teach them how to follow
Jesus in his words and deeds.
All that Jesus taught and did
has been written in the biblical Gospels.
Some time later, at Pentecost,
when many people from abroad
were present in Jerusalem,
the disciples received the Holy Spirit of God.
With the gift of the Holy Spirit
they told all present
about the coming kingdom of heaven.
And everyone understood the message,
no matter what country he or she came from.
After Pentecost, the apostles went into the world
with the good news of Jesus' message.

Jesus/'Isa

The messages to the people of Israel
from the time before Jesus were already
included in the Torah of Israel;
they are also included in the Bible,
together with the message of Jesus—the Gospel

—in the Qur'an called the Injil.

Letters and acts of the apostles (disciples)
are also included in the Bible.
The last book of the Bible mentions Jesus' revelation
to the apostle John.
In this book there is a description of how beautiful
everything will be when a new heaven and a new
   earth appear.
 Then God will wipe away all tears
from the eyes of all people who suffer
from pain and sadness.

Muhammad
(Surah 14:4)

Six centuries later,
Muhammad had to speak to the Arabs
Allah's words revealed to him by Jabra'il—
   Gabriel.
The messages to the people of Arabia
are written in the Qur'an.
The messengers went into the world
with this message.
To each nation, a messenger was sent,
speaking in the language of his own people,
to make things clear to them,
the Qur'an tells us (Surah 14:4).

And so the message from the Almighty
is passing through the world.
Nations hear the message in their
   own language
and pass it on
to their children and grandchildren
and to anyone who wants to hear it.

GOD IS GREAT!   ALLAHOU AKBAR!

Study Guide

Introduction to the Study Guide	164
1. The First Stories	173
Unit 1-A (All Children)	175
Unit 1-B (Christian Children)	178
1-B1 First Session	178
1-B2 Second Session	182
2. Ibrahim/Abraham	185
Unit 2-A (All Children)	187
Unit 2-B (Christian Children)	190
3. Ya'kub/Jacob	194
Unit 3 (All Children)	195
4 and 5. Musa/Moses and the Desert Journey	198
Units 4/5-A (All Children)	200
Units 4/5-B (Christian Children)	203
6. Guides, Judges, and Kings	207
Unit 6-A (All Children)	209
Unit 6-B (Christian Children)	212
7. The Births of Jesus/'Isa and John/Yahya	215
Unit 7 (All Children)	215
8. 'Isa/Jesus	220
Unit 8 (All Children)	221
Activities Instruction Section	
1. The First Stories	225
2. Ibrahim/Abraham	228
3. Ya'kub/Jacob	230
4 and 5. Musa/Moses and the Desert Journey	231
6. Guides, Judges, and Kings	233
7. The Births of Jesus/'Isa and John/Yahya	235
Reproducible Resources	237
Glossary	249

Introduction to the Study Guide

Muslims and Christians belong to storytelling communities. *Abraham and Ibrahim* focuses on figures known to both communities through the Bible and the Qur'an. The stories of these figures are an important common heritage shared by Christians and Muslims. Children, their parents, and their teachers will discover that the stories they know may be told differently in the other community. When this happens, they can discover something about what the story means in the other's tradition, thereby glimpsing another's view of God, the world, and human life. They may also find that, beyond the Qur'an and the Bible, there are other stories told by Muslims and Christians that reveal something about what each community values.

Islamic Sacred Narrative

"[The Qur'an's] mode of 'narrative' . . . emphasize[d] the common destiny of humankind . . . to serve one deity who required the creation of a public order that would reflect justice and harmony. Accordingly, the Islamic sacred narrative begins with the first human, Adam, who is regarded as history's first muslim (with a lower case 'm'; that is, a person who 'submits' to the will of God). Adam also marks the beginning of the human saga toward the creation of an ideal society on earth. . . . Thereafter, the Islamic narrative becomes part of the sacred narratives of the Old and New Testaments, reflecting the struggle of God's spokespersons sent to different communities in order to invite humankind to respond to their innate spiritual and moral dispositions. Finally, the narrative introduces the historical founder of Islam, the Prophet Muhammad."[1]

Using Resources for Study

Abraham and Ibrahim uses positioning on the page to indicate general sources: on the left, the Bible; on the right, the Qur'an. In the center, both the Qur'an and the Bible are the sources.

Christian and Muslim parents and teachers who wish to do so may obtain a copy of the other's scripture for use. Christians are cautioned that the verse numbering of the Qur'an is not consistent in all versions, so they may need to search surrounding verses of a citation. Further, names of persons and of the Divinity may either be in English or in the original Arabic. (*Abraham and Ibrahim* uses Arabic forms of names for Islamic sources. The study guide uses both English and Arabic forms interchangeably or in tandem. The honorifics, or titles used after names in Islamic practice, are not included.)

---

1. Abdulaziz Sachedina, "A Muslim Response," *Church & Society,* September–October 1992, p. 36.

Study Guide Contents

Abraham and Ibrahim is divided into eight units. The accompanying study guide offers the following aids for eight sessions to parents and teachers who are working with children in grades 3–8:

- Plans for groups of Christian children, with the objective of learning about and appreciating Islam while standing within their own Christian faith.
- Suggested discussion questions for groups made up of both Christian and Muslim children, intended to help them talk with one another about their religious traditions, beliefs, and practices.
- Boxes and notes with background for adult enrichment (and for possible selective use by gifted readers among the children).
- Activities Instruction Section, including directions and materials for a variety of activities.
- Reproducible Resources, including patterns, instructions and Scripture readings.

Leaders are urged to use the guide for their own reflection and learning as they prepare for working with children. Some notes in the guide are included solely for this purpose.

Preparation

The study guide is written to accommodate small groups of children but can be modified for use in a family setting with one or more children.

- Decide early how you will use *Abraham and Ibrahim*. Purchase and distribute the books.
- In a group in which all the children are competent readers, you might wish to distribute books to every child and ask that they read each unit before a session. This would allow the full time together to be spent in discussion and activities.
- In a group with some competent readers, you might ask one or more of these children to read the stories in a unit and, with adult assistance and prompting, to tell them to the whole group when it gathers (either in addition to or instead of an adult reading to the group).
- In all other situations, a parent or teacher should be asked to read (or tell) the stories at each session. Because only a part of each unit may be read when the group gathers, children will have a better experience if there is a book at home for family reading of the parts that will not be heard in the group gatherings.
- Develop a realistic time plan in advance.
- Story telling/reading should be confined to no more than one-third of session time and can cover key stories used in a session plan.

- All or some of the suggested discussion questions can be chosen, depending on the nature of the group and the time available.
- Activities should provide further learning opportunities. Select those that can interest the whole group. Consider cooperative work to accommodate differences in the children's skills. All children need not do the same activity.
- When you have decided which activities you will use, collect all necessary materials and run through each selected activity well in advance. Instructions for activities are found in the Activities Instruction Section, pages 224–236. Suggestions for finding material on the Web for activities and for use in the discussion period are offered in some cases. If you are not an Internet user, find someone who can help you.
- Plan how to adapt the discussion questions for your group. For younger children in particular, questions can be expanded to draw out concepts. For example, a question in Unit 2 asks how Abraham showed trust in God. It may be necessary to begin with one or more questions about trust in someone who is known to the children, such as a parent or a teacher, before moving to ask about Abraham's trust in God.
- Arrange your room so that it is a comfortable area for storytelling and discussion. Develop a plan for displaying charts, illustrations, and other materials. If possible, have an additional area available for handcraft activities.

Plans for Particular Types of Groups

Most children will need opportunities to reinforce learning the new information and concepts encountered in the sessions. As you proceed, themes you have already covered will reappear. For example, the theme of idolatry (first explored in Unit 2) will repeatedly recur. You can help children by briefly calling attention to this when appropriate. Likewise, there is sometimes an anticipation of themes that will only unfold in a future session. The first part of the *shahada*, the witness and confession of Muslims, is found in Unit 1 (in a presentation about the call to prayer) but the second part of the *shahada* is only presented in Unit 4.

If you discover that some of the children are far more able or willing to speak than others, be intentional about drawing all of them into the sessions. Ask yourself: Is there an age differential in the group that makes some feel uncomfortable? Are the children unfamiliar with one another? In a mixed group, are Christian children more invested in the discussion than Muslim children, or vice versa? Do some children feel that only adults should talk about religious matters and that they are expected to remain quiet? Does the approach of the lesson require more familiar material as a bridge into new information or new ideas?

For many of the units, separate plans for two types of groups are provided: a group with Muslim and Christian children and a group for Christian children only.

For Muslim and Christian children meeting together (marked as A plans)

Planning for a mixed group of Muslim and Christian children can best occur when there is at least one adult from each religious community involved in joint decision making. When you are ready, invite children to the group and give them details about the time and place of meeting, what preparation they should do in advance, if any, and what type of clothing you are expecting them to wear.

The discussion questions in the Study Guide suggest directions in which Christian and/or Muslim parents/teachers might lead children of both communities as they read *Abraham and Ibrahim* and talk together. The questions assume that the children know about their own religious community and its teachings sufficiently to talk about these with others. It will be important to allow children to speak for themselves without prompting as much as possible. When leaders see areas where the children's responses are confused or inaccurate, additional questions may help clarify what is being said. Be careful, however, to allow children to speak from within their own tradition. Islamic words in Arabic are provided in parentheses for the assistance of Christian teachers who want to help children connect with their tradition. Don't pressure Christian children to learn the Arabic vocabulary if this does not seem natural. Remember, too, that children may feel betrayed if an adult attempts to synthesize different viewpoints or experiences into some kind of commonality they do not feel.

Some regular opportunity for hospitality during your sessions will encourage conversation, whether or not the children have known each other previously. This might involve sharing special foods or customs or games together. If at all possible, find time to engage in some of the suggested activities described in the study guide. This will provide another venue in which children can talk and experience one another.

For Christian children (marked as B plans)

Session plans relate stories in *Abraham and Ibrahim* to Islamic practices and beliefs. The stories told in *Abraham and Ibrahim* do not solely constitute the central teachings of Islam. Muslim children are born into a community that teaches through example and involvement in the family, the mosque, and the larger environment. Islam emphasizes following a path of right living, according to God's will, and Muslims' beliefs are embodied in disciplined living. Therefore, the study guide offers suggestions for talking with Christian children about things Muslims experience. It also offers suggestions for activities that enable participatory learning.

> "A lot of what I learned was not verbal, but more integral to life."
> —*Comment on childhood learning about Islam from an American who grew up as a Christian in a Muslim society*

Introduction

Christian teachers and children are asked to engage in the suggested activities respectfully as follows:

- by treating the Bible and the Qur'an with care
- by disposing of the products of children's activities in cases where the children do not wish to keep what they have made, rather than allowing them to be tossed about
- by speaking about Muslims as though Muslims were present in the room, as a way of understanding that we live together in one world

In teaching Christian children about Islam, it is important to recognize that Muslims have many faces. As a significant portion of the world's population, they comprise the majority in over fifty nations. They stretch from Indonesia (the nation with the largest Muslim majority), to India (whose Muslim minority still comprises one of the largest Muslim populations in the world), to the Middle East (the homeland of Islam, where the Qur'an was revealed in Arabia), and on to Africa. There are Muslims in the United States who have come from many other nations during their own or their parents' lifetimes, as well as Muslims who have been in our land for many generations (particularly African Americans who have "reverted" to Islam). They share core practices and articles of faith. The practices and beliefs presented in the study guide plans include:

The five pillars of Islamic practice
- Reciting the confession of faith (Units 4 and 5)
- Praying (Unit 6)
- Contributing a proportion of one's wealth to charity (Unit 7)
- Fasting (Unit 8)
- Going on pilgrimage to Mecca (Unit 2)

Islamic beliefs
- God is One (Unit 1).
- God's prophets are messengers on earth (Unit 1).
- God revealed books to prophets (Unit 6).
- God is sovereign, i.e., everything is under the control of God (Unit 3).
- God wills the establishment of a just society on earth (Units 4 and 5).
- God will judge each human (Unit 8).

For teaching purposes, the stories of *Abraham and Ibrahim* are paired with these practices and beliefs.

Guidelines

A simple anecdote helps explain the basis for guidelines: A young American couple living in England found that English people often tried to make their acquaintance by chatting about differences between the English and

Americans—differences in vocabulary, differences in food preparation, differences in educational systems. The likenesses between the two peoples made such conversations easy but, while they provided good fillers at social occasions, they were rarely satisfying. Comparison, the couple discovered, was too facile. It allowed both them and their hosts to stay in their own mode of thinking and encouraged little real encounter. Consequently, the couple began searching for better ways to learn about England and the English through asking about things they did not understand or commenting on events around them; when they talked about American life, they did not invite comparisons. They began to develop more sustainable friendships.

The situation of the anecdote is not unlike that of persons of two religions—especially those of the same "family"—who are beginning to know one another. Several procedural guidelines can encourage sharing between Christian and Muslim children or adults:

- Accept the religious identity of each child, based upon the family and community in which the child is being raised.
- Refrain from conversations that simply look for similarities and differences between the two religions. Avoid unfair comparisons that look at the ideal best of "our" community but see the worst of "their" community.
- Listen to a community's stories—their versions of stories—as told by that community. Discover what each story means to the community that is telling it and how the story is used. Insofar as possible, set aside any comments or teachings about one community's stories that are made by the other community.
- Break stereotypical thinking by seeing the diversity among people in each community.

It is important to recognize that Western Christians wrote *Abraham and Ibrahim* and its study guide. No one ever fully stands within another's experiences, worldview, and spirituality. Thus it is our prayer that these resources may reflect, however imperfectly, the commandment of Jesus to love God with all our hearts and minds and to love our neighbors as ourselves.

The Qur'an and the Bible: Notes for Adults

The Qur'an is the holy book of Islam. The word "Qur'an" literally means "recitation": Muhammad recited to his followers the words revealed to him in the seventh century C.E. The words were collected into a book, the Qur'an, which is revered as the record of the very words of God. Accordingly, great respect is given to the Qur'an. It is placed on a stand so it will not be on the floor where people walk. It is often stored on the highest shelf so nothing will be above it. Muslims wash themselves before touching it.

Introduction

The literary form of the Qur'an is unequalled and, indeed, is considered by Muslims to be a miracle. Because of its uniqueness, the Qur'an cannot be translated from Arabic but is only interpreted in other languages, in versions that help readers understand it. The Qur'an is often heard in beautiful recitation that uniquely conveys its words. All Muslims are expected to learn to say prayers and recite simply from the Qur'an in Arabic. Arabic calligraphy of Qur'anic verses is the visual form of its divine revelation. Inscriptions on mosques are from the Qur'an. Much Islamic art is in the form of beautiful calligraphy.

The Qur'an recognizes that "books" were given to other prophets, for their own people, before the revelation to Muhammad. Muslims consider the Qur'an to be for all people—the perfection of the "previous scriptures."

The Bible is the holy book of Christians that contains the writings commonly described as the Old and New Testaments, composed and collected over many centuries. Muslims use Arabic words for parts of the Bible: the *Tawrat* (the Torah), the *Zabur* (the Psalms), and the *Injil* (the Gospel). Although Muslims show reverence to the Bible, many Muslims consider it to have been corrupted in transmission (Surah 2:75, 78).

Christians say that the Bible's many authors were "inspired by the Holy Spirit" to tell about the works and revelation of God in human words, although they recognize that the Bible contains direct words of God within it. Christians call the Bible the "Word of God" because it is a means by which God has communicated with humans, but they particularly speak of Jesus as "the Word" (John 1:1ff.).

The Bible was written in three different languages: the Old Testament in Hebrew and Aramaic, and the New Testament in Greek. Jews share with Christians the text of what Christians call the Old Testament, although they possess a unique history of interpretation of that text and maintain the regular reading of it in the Hebrew language. Most Christians believe that the Bible can be understood through translation. The Hebrew Scriptures were translated early into Greek, even before the time of Jesus. Jesus' teachings have not been preserved in the language he spoke, Aramaic, but were translated into Greek before they were recorded in the New Testament. Generally only Christian scholars and religious leaders learn to read the Bible in Hebrew and Greek.

Since Christians are familiar with the Bible in their own languages, they use the translated form of names that are in the Bible. In English translations, "Jesus" is used, not the Hebrew "Yehoshua" nor the Greek "Iesus." Translations into other languages use other forms: "Jezus" in Dutch, "Yesus" in Indonesian, "Yesu" in Swahili, "Jesu" in Tagalog, or "Isa" in Turkish. Likewise, "God" is used by English speakers, while Arab Christians use "Allah," Persian or Urdu speakers use "Khoda," and Spanish speakers say "Dios." God is often called "LORD" in English translations; this is used where there is a special name for God in Hebrew.

Pronouns for God vary in different languages. Arabic, as a language that has gender, speaks of Allah as masculine, and Muslims retain this in whatever language they speak. Christians tend to deal with the gender in which they speak about God according to the customs of particular languages into which the Bible is translated.

The Arabic form of Qur'anic names is very similar to the Hebrew form of names found in the Bible; for example, "Ya'kub" (Jacob) in Arabic is very like "Yakov" in Hebrew. Translated Bible names are commonly used by Christians when they speak or when they name their children, but many Muslims regularly use Arabic forms—whether in telling the story of Ibrahim (Hebrew, "Avraham," or English, "Abraham") or in naming a child Ibrahim.

Unit 1

The First Stories

The Big Ideas
The stories: Creation, Adam and Eve, Noah
The concepts: languages of scripture; hiddenness
The belief/practice: God is One.

Creation to Noah: Notes for Adults
God is the one Creator of heaven and earth, as attested in both the Bible and the Qur'an. Creation is by God's word. The creation of humans—the aspect of creation most extensively described in the Qur'an—takes place last. While the Qur'an says that to create heaven and earth is greater than creating humankind (Surah 40:57), it considers everything on earth to be created for humanity (Surah 2:29), especially animals (Surah 16:5). The Bible speaks of humans having "dominion" over the animals (Genesis 1:26). Creation is considered in the Bible to be the beginning of God's acts in history to fulfill God's purpose for humanity (Romans 8:19–23). Adam is called in the Qur'an a "vicegerent" (*khalifa*), that is, one who represents God to do God's will on earth (Surah 2:30).

In both the Hebrew of the Bible and the Arabic of the Qur'an, the name of the first person, Adam, can be translated as "human" or "humankind." The "offspring of Adam," *bani adam*, can be interpreted as "everyone." Adam was made from dust or clay into which God breathed God's spirit, to give life. In Hebrew, the word "Adam" is related to the word for "ground."

The story of Adam in the Bible is not just the story of one man; it is, in a very real sense, the story of humankind. Humanity is created in the "image of God." This is not interpreted to be physical resemblance in any sense, but rather refers to the ability of humans to communicate with God. Adam is made for community, shown by God's provision of a partner, Eve, so that Adam will not be alone. Adam has a special role in creation as the one who can name all animals and have certain control over them.

In the Qur'an, when God creates Adam, God orders the angels to bow down to Adam; Adam has authority over all creation, including the angels (Surahs 2:30ff.; 7:11ff.; 15:26ff.; 17:61ff.; 20:116). The refusal of one angel to bow down to Adam brings about the angel's downfall and he, as the devil, tempts Adam. This leads to Adam's sin and Adam's expulsion from the garden, Eden. God attributes Adam's sin to weakness and God guides Adam into the right way (Surah 20:114–128).

The Hebrew Scriptures' narrative about Adam indicates that God's purpose for humanity is that humans live in fellowship with God and in obedient service in the world. Adam's sin is disobeying God. Adam thereby breaks his close relationship with God. In the New Testament, Adam is seen as the one through whom sin—the source of death—entered into the world. In contrast, Christ, "the last Adam," gives grace and life (Romans 5:12–21).

Adam has a high status in the Qur'an and, in tradition, is even associated with Mecca, the place to which Muslims go on pilgrimage to this day.

Noah is honored in both the Bible and the Qur'an. In the Bible he is not only the hero who saved all living things and humanity from the flood, but also a righteous man who had faith in God and obeyed God (Ezekiel 14:14, 20; Hebrews 11:7; 2 Peter 2:5). In the Qur'an, Noah is considered a prophet with the same status as Abraham, Moses, Jesus, and Muhammad (Surah 42:13). He is particularly honored as the one who warned the people to worship God and to escape from the punishment of the flood and who endured their taunts and rejection (Surah 71). As such, Noah is a model for all the prophets who came after him.

Study Guide

Materials Needed
- Bible
- Qur'an
- Hebrew and/or Greek Bible (*optional*)
- Newsprint
- Markers
- Photocopies of "Information about Muslim Writing" (page 237) (*optional*)
- Green chenille stems (*optional*)
- Materials to make lamps (see page 226) (*optional*)
- Hymnals (*optional*)
- Cassette tape of the Muslim call to prayer (see page 227) (*optional*)
- Tape player (*optional*)

Unit 1-A: Muslim and Christian Children Together

Before the class begins and before beginning the plans listed, you may want to devise your own plans for an introductory get-acquainted session. You could use ideas from the beginning of 1-B1 on talking about personal names and from the Introductory Questions below. Read aloud the Introduction (page 1) to close an introductory session.

If you are not doing a get-acquainted session, use all the plans here in a single session, taking time at the beginning to share names and other personal information.

Preparation
Have newsprint paper and a marker ready for use. Arrange a place in the room for displaying the sheet(s) of paper for each future session.

Introductory Questions
Discuss the questions with your class before reading from the book.

- We are going to talk about stories found in our holy books, the Bible and the Qur'an. Do you have one of these books at home? Do you take care of it in some special way? How? Why?
- Do you know in what languages the Bible was originally written? In what language is the Qur'an written?

Show your class a copy of the Qur'an in Arabic, with or without a parallel interpretive translation into English. Then show a Bible in English (include Bibles in other contemporary languages, if available). Also show the Hebrew Old Testament and the Greek New Testament if you have access to them.

- Christians usually say the word "God" in their own language. Can you tell us what the word is in any language besides English? Muslims use the Arabic word "Allah." In what other ways do Muslims use Arabic? Why?
- We will be talking about a lot of people whose stories are in the Qur'an and the Bible. We may find we have different ways of pronouncing their names. If you use these names, will you help me say the names the way you do?

Unit 1: The First Stories

Hearing the Stories

Before class, read through the stories for Unit 1. All the stories for Unit 1 should be read aloud to the children. You may choose to read all the story portions you have selected before beginning discussion, or you may decide to break up the discussion by talking about each section immediately after reading it.

Before reading the stories, ask the children to listen for names or descriptions we use for God, so that you can make a list of them on newsprint (be ready to add to it throughout the discussion time and save it for future sessions).

As you get input from both Christian and Muslim children, there is no need to separate their responses on your list, but be aware of any differences in approach so that they can be addressed as needed. Do not attempt to combine various responses into one, but do avoid recording repeat contributions more than once.

After you read out loud the stories from Unit 1, ask the following questions.

- What are some names for God/Allah that we have heard today? Let's make our list (e.g., Almighty, Our Sovereign, Creator, Lord, the First and the Last). Today did we hear anything more about God that belongs on our list? (Encourage listing only names and attributes found in the Unit 1 reading.)
- Allah/God created light (Surah 6:1; Genesis 1:3ff.). Muslims and Christians both use lights in their places of worship. Are there candles or lamps or special lights in the place where your family worships (either at home or in a church/mosque)? Where are they? Why do you think people use these special lights? What do they tell us about God/Allah and about ourselves?

Share the following story that tells us something about God and about ourselves:

In Iran and Turkey and some other countries, there are stories about a man who is called Mullah Nasruddin by Iranians. It is said that one day Mullah Nasruddin was seen down on his hands and knees, looking for his ring in the middle of a road. Others came to help him look, and when they could not find the ring, they asked, "Mullah, are you sure that this is where you lost your ring?" Mullah answered, pointing, "No, no. I lost my ring over there." "Then, why," the people asked, "are you looking for your ring here?" "It's too dark over there. There is more light in this place," he replied, "so I thought we might have more success looking here."

Do not feel compelled to over-analyze this Mullah Nasruddin story. Let it speak for itself.

Study Guide

- ❓ The first humans ate fruit from a tree from which God had told them not to eat. What did God do then? What do we learn about God/Allah from the way they were treated?
- ❓ Muslims call both Adam and Nuh "prophets." One of the tasks of a prophet (*nabi*) is to warn people. How did Nuh/Noah warn people? How did the people respond? Do you think Allah/God warns people like us today? How?

Activities

See Activities Instruction Section for instructions and resources for the activities in the unit (pages 224–236). Devise your own plan for the session, using these activities at the end of the session or during an earlier part of the session when they can be connected directly to the particular part of the conversation to which they relate.

- Christian children, with the help of their Muslim friends, can learn to identify the word "Allah" in Arabic script by going through the process of forming it out of a chenille stem. The word "Allah" in Arabic can be found on page 225. The reproducible pages "Information about Muslim Writing" (pages 237–238) provide the children information about Arabic script.
- Make a model of a light that would be used in the mihrab of a mosque or draw pictures of candles or other special lights in a church. See page 226 for instructions and a list of materials needed.
- Listen to a recording of the Muslim call to prayer and talk about its words, "There is no god except God." See page 227 for details. (Save discussion of any additional words in the call to prayer until later.)
- Read or sing out loud "All Things Bright and Beautiful," a Christian hymn about creation. If they know it, the Christian children can sing the hymn for their friends. It can be found in *The Presbyterian Hymnal*, no. 267.

For the Next Session

Ask children to be ready for the next session, in accordance with your prepared plans. Do they need to read parts of the book at home? Do they need to bring anything? Be sure you tell parents what is needed, preferably in writing.

Look ahead to Unit 2, and gather any items needed for the activities. Read through the activities carefully, as some will need advance preparation.

Unit 1: The First Stories

Materials Needed
- Newsprint
- Markers
- Cassette tape of a Muslim call to prayer
- Tape player
- Dictionary
- Construction paper
- Felt-tipped markers or crayons
- Photocopies of "Information about Muslim Writing" (pages 237–238)
- Green chenille stems
- Hymnals

Unit 1-B: Christian Children

You will use two sessions to cover Unit 1. Do any needed introductory orientation in the first session. Later, in Unit 2, the children will talk about the words "Islam" and "Muslim." In the meantime, model appropriate usage by remembering that Muslims are people and Islam is their religion.

Unit 1-B1: *First Session*

Preparation

Plan display space for (1) a list of names/attributes of God, (2) brief descriptions about what has been learned about Islam, and (3) illustrative pictures and products of the children's activities. Write out the words to the *Bismillah* (see page 227) on a piece of newsprint and display it where the children can see it.

Have newsprint paper and a marker ready for making the list of names of God.

Suggested Introductory Questions

Invite the children to share their names and what they know about their names. Is it a name that someone else in the family had? Is it a name from the Bible? In what language(s) is the name commonly used?

Talk about names used in the United States that are in different languages but come from the same source; for example, Maria in Spanish, Mary in English, Maryam in Arabic, Miriam in Hebrew.

Share that you will be reading a book, *Abraham and Ibrahim*, about people in the Bible and in the holy book of Muslims, the Qur'an. The book's title comes from a name in two different languages, Abraham (English) and Ibrahim (Arabic). These names are given to babies in the United States today.

- How would a family decide which form of the name to give? Why? (Be aware that culture may play a role in the children's answers, as well as religion.)
- Muslims read about Ibrahim in Arabic because their holy book is in Arabic. In what language was the Christian holy book, the Bible, written? In Hebrew, Abraham's name is Avraham.

Invite the children to look at samples of Arabic writing found below.

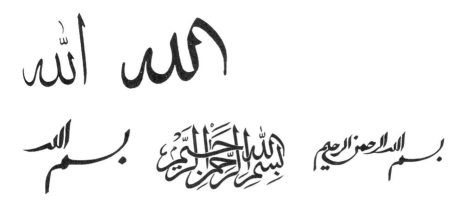

❷ Do we read the Bible in Greek or Hebrew? In what language do we read the Bible?

This is because Christians translate the Bible and use it in their own languages. Muslims do not translate the Qur'an, although they may have an interpretation in their own language to read after they have heard it recited in Arabic. (Use the notes in the box "The Qur'an and the Bible" on pages 169–171 for background information.)

❷ The Bible is a special book. Do you treat it in any special way?

Talk about Muslims giving great importance to the Qur'an and treating it in special ways.

Hearing the Stories
Read out loud the Introduction (page 1) and the Unit 1 section "The Creator and the Creation" (pages 3–7). Invite the class to listen for the things these sections tell us about God or Allah, including names used for God (e.g., Almighty, the First and the Last, Wise). After the reading, make a list of the names on newsprint. When the session is over, display your list and save it for later use.

Share that the Qur'an begins with some words about God that are written in it over and over. They are "In the name of God, the Merciful, the Compassionate" (Surah 1:1), known as the *Bismillah*. Muslims repeat these words at the beginning of their prayers, before they read the Qur'an, and before they begin a new activity. The words are also put at the top of written materials.

❷ What do we learn about God from these words used by Muslims? Are "Merciful" and "Compassionate" on our list of names for God?

Ask the class to think about when they might say or write "In the name of God" if they were following that particular custom (e.g., at the top of a letter to Grandma, when they start to eat, when they start to give a report in their school classroom).

If the children sense that there is some connection to times when Christians say grace, pray in Jesus' name, and so on, allow them to talk about this.

Say to the class: We have made a list of names used for God. The most important thing Muslims say is about God. They say, "There is no god except God" (Surah 47:19). If you lived in a place where there were many Muslims, you would hear these words called at different times throughout the day from the minaret, a tower beside the mosque, the Muslim place of worship.

If you have obtained a recording of the call to prayer, use it now (see the Web addresses given in the Activities Instruction Section on page 227). Show the illustration of a minaret on page 181.

Today the call to prayer may be broadcast by loudspeaker or even radio and television. The call usually includes the words "God is greater. I witness that there is no god except God. I witness that Muhammad is the messenger of God. Come to prayer." Focus on the words about God in this session.

Muslims emphasize that there is nothing else and no one else like God. They say, "God is One," which means that God is unique. Think together about the word "unique," looking it up in a dictionary, as may be needed.

❷ How can we talk about God if there is no one else like God, who is unique?
❷ Muslims believe God is both near to us and far from us. The Qur'an says that God is closer to humans than their jugular vein (Surah 50:16). Where is our jugular vein? Does this make God known and familiar or unknown and unfamiliar? The Qur'an also calls God "the Unseen" (Surah 6:50). Does this make God known and familiar, or unknown and unfamiliar? Why?

Tell the story of Mullah Nasruddin (page 176), a story told by some Muslims.

Activities (See Activities Instruction Section for details.)
- Have the class write the words of the *Bismillah,* which may be done in many shapes and many scripts (see page 227). Pass out construction paper and markers or crayons.
- Make the shape of the word "Allah" out of chenille stems (see Activities Instruction Section, page 225). See "Information about Muslim Writing" (pages 237–238) for an illustration of the word "Allah" in Arabic, as well as more information about Arabic writing.

Closing
Listen to or sing the hymn "All Things Bright and Beautiful" about creation. The hymn can be found in *The Presbyterian Hymnal*, no. 267. At the end of the listening time, you might wish to lead the children in short prayers of thanks for God's creation.

For the Next Session
Look ahead to the second session for Unit 1 and decide what activities the class will do. You will need to find pictures of different forms of Islamic dress from around the world.

A minaret is a tall, slender tower of a mosque. The call to prayer is cried from its balcony.

Unit 1: The First Stories

> **Materials Needed**
> ☐ Newsprint
> ☐ Markers
> ☐ Pictures of Islamic dress (see "Hearing the Stories" below)
> ☐ Cassette tape of a Muslim call to prayer (see page 227)
> ☐ Tape player
> ☐ Crayons
> ☐ Felt-tipped markers
> ☐ Pencils

Unit 1-B2: *Second Session*

Preparation
Before class, post the list about God from the previous session in a place where you can write additions on it.

Suggested Introductory Questions
Review what you did in the previous session, particularly calling to mind any parts of the conversation or the activity period you think were key or that excited the children.

❷ We talked last time about God being as near as our jugular vein but also being "the Unseen." We will be reading more of the stories in *Abraham and Ibrahim* today. Before reading, let's think about an idea we will hear in the stories. It is about when *we* try to be unseen, about hiding. Did you ever play hide and seek? Why was it fun to be where others could not see you?

❷ Now think of times when you disobeyed and wanted to hide so that your mother or your father or your teacher or your friend would not discover you and see that you had done something wrong. How did you feel? Think about the ways you felt at these different times as you listen to the stories.

Hearing the Stories
Read or tell the class the sections on "Humankind" through "Nuh/Noah" (pages 9–20).

Tell the children that you are ready to add things about God to the newsprint list if they heard something they want to put on it.

❷ After Adam and Eve ate from the tree from which God asked them not to eat, they saw that they were naked and sewed leaves to cover themselves. Were they trying to hide? From whom?

Adam and Eve clothed themselves. Talk about ways that people have observed modesty, or not, since early times. One of the characteristics of all Muslims is that they have been taught by the Qur'an to be modest (Surah 24:30f.). This includes both women and men.

If you have pictures available, look at different forms of Islamic dress around the world and notice the different ways that Muslims interpret the teaching that they be modest. It is important to note that not all Muslim women cover their heads but that many do, including many women who make this decision themselves in societies where women have free choice.

Notice that Muslim men do not ordinarily appear in public in shorts or other minimal clothing.

- In what ways are you modest? Why do you do these things? Can we hide from God? Should we hide some things from other people?

With older children who may be aware of current events, talk about the Qur'an quote from Surah 5:32 at the bottom of page 14 and the top of page 15. In the story told in "The First Sons," there were two brothers and one of them, Cain, killed the other. Do you think Cain wanted to hide? From whom? Did God let him hide? Why do you think God did not allow Cain to be killed as a punishment for killing his brother? What do you think was Cain's responsibility when God saved him from being killed? Can you give an example of a recent murder that you believe God did not want to happen? What example can you give of someone saving the life of another person?

If you are not using this question and your time schedule is tight, you may skip the reading of "The First Sons," depending on the time available.

- Look at the Noah story. What did God tell Noah to do? What did Noah tell other people? What does the story in the Qur'an say about the way other people treated Noah? How did Noah respond? Did he hide from other people or stay where he would be seen? Why?
- The Qur'an calls Noah a prophet (*nabi*)—one who warned against evil. What other prophets were mentioned at the end of the story of Noah as we have heard it read? Can you think of ways that Moses warned people? How did Jesus warn people? (We will hear more about both Moses and Jesus later.)

According to Islam, God sent many prophets. The Qur'an's list of prophets may surprise the children. It may be useful to recall the figures represented in the Old Testament prophetic books and in the history of Israel (starting with Samuel) and to think about whether they were "warners." Be careful not to think of a prophet as someone who primarily tells the future, a common modern definition of the term.

- How do we react today when someone warns us about anything? Think of some times when a whole group of people or a whole country gets a warning (e.g., about a coming storm). How would you react if you were told a warning came directly from God? Does God, in fact, give warnings today? How?

Unit 1: The First Stories

Activities (See Activities Instruction Section for details.)
- Have the class recall some important things about Islam and Muslims that they have learned in this session and in the first session. Make a chart or a series of signs that briefly list these things. Post them in your room. Add to the chart or make additional signs as you learn new things in future sessions.

  If you do not do this as a children's activity, plan to make a chart yourself on which you include brief descriptions of what the class has learned. Post the chart regularly in your room as a reminder for the children.
- Listen again to the Muslim call to prayer to which you listened in the previous session. A part of its words are "There is no god except God." What have you heard in the stories from *Abraham and Ibrahim* that emphasizes this message?
- Have the children imagine the Garden of Eden and what God would have placed in it. Make a mural or have them draw individual pictures and tell each other about their pictures. (This activity could be continued by asking each child to imagine how the picture would be changed by the garden's perfection being spoiled through not doing as God asked.)

For the Next Session

Ask children to be ready for the next session, in accordance with your plans. Do they need to read at home? Do they need to bring anything? Be sure you tell parents what is needed, preferably in writing.

Look ahead to Unit 2, and gather any items needed for the activities. Make sure to read through the activities carefully, as some will need advance preparation.

Unit 2

Ibrahim/ Abraham

The Big Ideas
The story: Abraham
The concept: idolatry
The belief/practice: pilgrimage

> **Abraham and His Sons: Notes for Adults**
> Jews, Christians, and Muslims honor Abraham. Abraham has a special relationship with God and is called "the friend of God" in both the Bible and the Qur'an (Isaiah 41:8; Surah 4:125). The Qur'an portrays Abraham, the friend of God, as the leader of those who commit themselves to God. Abraham is recognized in the Bible as a mediator and intercessor with God: through his intercession God rescued Lot (Genesis 19:29) and, by the Israelites' appeal to the promises God made to Abraham, God's wrath was turned from them in the wilderness (Exodus 32:13).
>
> Abraham is understood by Christians to be the father of the Israelite and Christian communities (Isaiah 51:2, Galatians 3:29) and all people of faith (Galatians 3:7). Jesus' words indicate, however, that this is not a simple matter of ancestral lineage (Matthew 3:9f., Luke 3:8f.); the Bible emphasizes Abraham as the figure of faith and, therefore, the model for all the faithful.
>
> In particular, Abraham is remembered as the one who—having waited patiently for the fulfillment of God's promise that he should have a son and many descendants—was nevertheless prepared to be obedient when he heard God call him to sacrifice his son.
>
> The universal legacy of Abraham's life is indicated in the Qur'an by his role as the founder, together with his son Ishmael (Surah 2:125), of the holy Ka'ba in Mecca as the house of worship for all humankind (Surah 3:96). According to the Qur'an some of the events in the life of Abraham took place in the vicinity of Mecca. These events are reenacted in the rituals of the annual pilgrimage, or *hajj*, that Muslim faithful make to Mecca.

Unit 2: Ibrahim/Abraham

The Bible speaks of both sons of Abraham. God made an everlasting covenant with the descendants of Abraham through Isaac and a promise to bless Abraham's son Ishmael and is descendants (Genesis 17:19–21). The relationship of the two sons to one another is noted in the Bible. They played together, thereby causing the jealousy of Abraham's wife, Sarah (Genesis 21:9). Isaac, the child born according to the Spirit in the New Testament (Galatians 4:28–29), is said to have been persecuted by "the child born according to the flesh"—that is, Ishmael. Both sons are called prophets in the Qur'an (Surah 19:49). Nothing about their relationship with one another is mentioned, though their names are together in lists of prophets and messengers.

The call to Abraham to sacrifice his son is highlighted in both the Bible and the Qur'an. The son of the sacrifice is named in the Bible as Isaac but is unnamed in the Qur'an; most Muslim scholars consider the son to be Ishmael.

Materials Needed
- ❏ Bible (*optional*)
- ❏ Children's book on Malcolm X (see page 189) (*optional*)
- ❏ Materials for the Ka'ba Cube (see page 228)
- ❏ Photocopies of "Cube Pattern" (page 239) (*optional*)
- ❏ Photocopies of "Math in Muslim Thought" (page 240) (*optional*)
- ❏ Christmas or Easter decorations or materials for Christmas or Easter craft (see page 189)
- ❏ Photocopies of "Postage Stamps" (pages 241–242) (*optional*)
- ❏ Crayons or felt-tipped markers

Unit 2-A: Muslim and Christian Children Together

Preparation
Arrange the seating in the room, so that the children can see the book as you read out loud. If you choose to have Christmas or Easter decorations, put them on display where the children can see them.

Suggested Introductory Questions
❷ In the time of Ibrahim there were many idols. What is an idol?

Read the story "Ibrahim/Abraham" (pages 23–24) to the children. Ask, What do you think the idols were like?

Retell the story in this way: One day the people of Ibrahim's tribe went away from home, but Ibrahim stayed behind. While the others were away, he went to the nearby temple of the gods. With an axe, he cut off parts of some of the idols, and then put the axe in the hand of the biggest idol. When the others came back, they went to the temple and saw what had happened. They said Ibrahim had done it! But Ibrahim answered, "No, the biggest of the gods did this. If they can talk, ask them." The others replied, "You know they can't speak." Then Ibrahim said to them, "Do you worship what cannot help you and disregard Allah?" (Based on Surah 21:58–67.)[2]

❷ What does this story tell us about the idols? How is God/Allah different from the idols in this story?

❷ If you wish, read out loud Jeremiah 10:6–16. How is God different from idols (things created by people) in this passage?

The Hajj
The pilgrimage (*hajj*) to Mecca, which takes place in the Islamic lunar month of Dhu al-Hijja, is a demonstration of Islamic unity as Muslims from all over the world gather in one place to worship the one God together. In 2004, over two and a half million Muslims from 160 countries participated. The pilgrimage is a requirement of Islamic practice. At least once in his or her lifetime, every able-bodied Muslim who can afford to go must go.

---

2. Adapted from "Ibrahim," *The Shorter Encyclopedia of Islam* (Ithaca, NY: Cornell University Press, 1974), p. 54.

Unit 2: Ibrahim/Abraham

"When Muslims make the pilgrimage to Mecca, they find the Abrahamic elements of their religion brought to life for their imaginations. All pilgrims dress in similar white garments of ancient style to remind them of the time of Abraham. They do homage at the Ka'ba, the ancient shrine on the spot where they believe that Abraham built the first House of God. They walk seven times between two hills in the city in memory of Hagar, repudiated by Abraham, who is believed to have run back and forth there in search of water for herself and for her son, Ishmael. They draw water from the well of Zamzam, reputed to be the source of water miraculously provided for the mother and son. The multitudes of pilgrims throw stones at a masonry pillar in the Valley of Mina to commemorate Abraham's rejection of satanic temptations. Then on the tenth day of the month . . . [they] sacrifice an animal in memory of Abraham's willingness to sacrifice his son in obedience to the command of God."[3]

❓ The Muslim holiday 'Id al-Adha, the Feast of Sacrifice, is a remembrance of Abraham's sacrifice of an animal in place of his son. How do you celebrate this day? This day is celebrated at a time when many Muslims are on pilgrimage (*hajj*) to Mecca. What do you know about what they are doing there on 'Id al-Adha?

> 'Id al-Adha is on the tenth of the month of Dhu al-Hijja in a lunar calendar, so it rotates between the seasons of the solar calendar used in the United States.

You may want to talk about Muslims' donating meat to assist the poor at the time of the feast.

❓ The Qur'an tells about Ibrahim and his son building a place for worship in Mecca. This is where Muslims go on the *hajj* pilgrimage. What is a pilgrimage? Can you describe what Muslims do when they go to Mecca on pilgrimage?

Allow the children to speak but, if they are unable to answer, assist them, perhaps even with a prepared chart. See "The Hajj" (page 187) for information.

❓ The *hajj* pilgrimage is the most important time when Muslims show that they all worship God in the same way, no matter where in the world they live. How do people who go on pilgrimage show that they are all equal before God?

❓ What are holidays when Christians remember things that happened in the stories of the Bible? What things in the celebrations help Christians to remember the stories?

3. R. Marston Speight, *God Is One: The Way of Islam*, 2nd ed. (New York: Friendship Press, 1989), pp. 42–44.

- Why is Abraham's son Ishmael important to Muslims? Why is Abraham's son Jacob/Israel important to Christians? How did God show favor to Abraham's descendants?
- Christians emphasize that God promised Abraham that his descendants would be a "blessing" to all people. What is a blessing? How do Christians believe the descendants became a blessing? (Be sure the children understand the concepts of ancestor and descendant.)
- In the Bible, we are told that God honored Abraham for his faith. In what ways did Abraham show he trusted God by the way he lived? How do people today show that they trust God?

Activities (See Activities Instruction Section for details.)
- *The Autobiography of Malcolm X* described the effect of the *hajj* upon him. Look for a children's book about Malcolm X in the library and read about his going on pilgrimage to Mecca. If a child has read about Malcolm in advance, ask for a report. Find a way to show what has been learned.
- Have the children look at a picture of the Ka'ba. Have them make a cube (see page 228) to remind them of the Ka'ba.
- Pass out copies of "Math in Muslim Thought" (page 240). Follow the directions in the Activities Instructions Section, page 229, for this exercise.
- Bring something with religious significance (or ask children to bring something) that Christians use to celebrate Christmas, Easter, or some other holiday that is related to a Bible story. Have the Christian children share what the items are, when they are used and how they are used. Make something related to one of these holidays, if appropriate.

- Pass out copies of "Postage Stamps" (pages 241–242) and have the children look at the reproduction of the Eid postage stamp printed by the U.S. Postal Service; look at one or more Christmas stamps with a religious theme. Talk about why the U.S. Postal Service might issue stamps to celebrate both religious events. Pass out copies of the stamps and crayons or markers. Have the children color the stamps.

For the Next Session
Ask children to be ready for the next session, in accordance with your prepared plans. Do they need to read parts of the book at home? Do they need to bring anything? Be sure you tell parents what is needed, preferably in writing.

The next unit contains one session that can be used for all children. You will need to find a picture of a *tasbih* (a string of beads Muslims use to recite the Ninety-nine Names of God). If you work with a class of Christian and Muslim children, invite your Muslim students to bring a *tasbih*. You may also try to find a rosary or a picture of one.

Unit 2: Ibrahim/Abraham

Materials Needed
- ☐ Modeling clay
- ☐ Dictionary
- ☐ Children's book on Malcolm X
- ☐ Newsprint
- ☐ Crayons or markers
- ☐ Materials to make Ka'ba (see page 228)
- ☐ Photocopies of "Cube Pattern" (page 239) (*optional*)

Unit 2-B: Christian Children

Preparation
You will want the students to sit in a circle where they can see the book you'll be reading about Malcolm X. Display the newsprint charts from previous sessions where you can easily write on them.

Suggested Introductory Questions
Have your class look together at the list of names/descriptions for God they made in the previous sessions. Share that you are going to read the story of Abraham today. Invite the children to listen for ways that Abraham tried to encourage others to worship God/Allah.

You may omit the reading of the last two sections of Unit 2. Note that the portion of "The Sons of Ibrahim/Abraham" on the giving of the Qur'an relates to material that will be visited for discussion in the Units 4/5 session.

❷ What do you think the idols in the time of Abraham were like?

Read "Ibrahim/Abraham" on pages 23–24 out loud. Ask your students to share what they think idols were like after hearing the story.

Retell the story using the following: One day the people of Ibrahim's tribe went away from home, but Ibrahim stayed behind. While the others were away, he went to the nearby temple of the gods. With an axe, he cut off parts of some of the idols, and then put the axe in the hand of the biggest idol. When the others came back, they went to the temple and saw what had happened. They said Ibrahim had done it! But Ibrahim answered, "No, the biggest of the gods did this. If they can talk, ask them." The others replied, "You know they can't speak." Then Ibrahim said to them, "Do you worship what cannot help you and disregard Allah?" (based on Surah 21:58–67).[4]

❷ How did Ibrahim help others see what the idols were really like? What does this story tell us about the idols? How is God/Allah different from the idols in this story?

You may wish to use modeling clay to make a very rough shape that you describe as an idol that cannot speak or hear.

❷ Do you think idols are always made of wood or stone or clay?

4. Ibid.

- One place in the New Testament (Colossians 3:5) says that greed is idolatry, that is, worshiping idols. What does it mean to be greedy? Does this give you a different idea about what an idol can be? Is an idol anything that keeps us from worshiping God? In what ways can greed keep us from worshiping God?

In Islam, idolatry (*shirk*) is making anything equal to God, that is, worshiping anything or anybody besides God. Remember that Muslims say, "There is no god but God."

- What might be an idol today? Are there some things that we make more important than anything or anybody else?
- The word "Muslim" is an Arabic word. It means a person who "submits" to God. The word "Islam" is an Arabic word for the religion of Muslims (and means "submission"). What can "submitting to God" mean? Is it the same as obeying God? Is it doing what God wants and, in this way, behaving as a person who believes "there is no god but God"?
- In what ways did Abraham submit to God?

> **Shirk: A Note for Adults**
> Guarding against *shirk*—the association of anything with God—has led to considerable disagreement within Islam itself (for example, concerning whether it is acceptable to venerate saints). Outside their own community, Muslims have difficulty with the Christian view of the Trinity (see, e.g., Surahs 4:171–172; 5:116–119; 23:91). One North American Muslim has written, "[I]f God is three persons or possesses three parts, He is assuredly not the Single, Unique, Indivisible Being which God is and which Christianity professes to believe in. To Muslims this makes absolutely no sense. . . . [B]elief in the trinity is regarded by Islam . . . as a form of polytheism."[5]

- The Qur'an tells about Abraham and his son building the Ka'ba in Mecca (a city in what we now call Saudi Arabia). Later, the Ka'ba became a place for worshiping idols. Muhammad returned it to being a place for worship of Allah. One of the things that Muslims do today is to go on pilgrimage to this place. What is a pilgrimage?

Use the dictionary with the children, if necessary, to find the generic definition of pilgrimage. Then share the following information about the pilgrimage to Mecca.

---

5. Suzanne Haneef, *What Everyone Should Know about Islam and Muslims* (Chicago: Kazi Publications, 1996), p. 207.

Unit 2: Ibrahim/Abraham

Going to Mecca is something that Muslims from all over the world do together. All the people of Islam are part of one community (the *umma*). When Muslims are together on pilgrimage (the *hajj*), they are all equal. To show this, all the men wear the same kind of very simple white clothing; all the women also wear very simple white clothing.

Using the information in "The Hajj," pages 187–188, as background information, tell the children about what Muslims do on the pilgrimage and connect these things to Abraham's life. If you have pictures, show the children scenes from the *hajj*. See the Activities Instruction Section, page 229, for possible sources.

- How do you think the activities of the pilgrimage would help Muslims remember that they are to submit to God?
- How does being together help people to worship God and submit to God? (The "Activities" section below suggests learning about Malcolm X. If you have planned ahead for this activity, you may wish to connect it to this discussion about the equality of all pilgrims.)
- What things do Christians do together?

Muslims who do not go on pilgrimage to Mecca share the celebration of the Day of Sacrifice, known as 'Id al-Adha, with all the Muslims who celebrate in Mecca (on the tenth day of the pilgrimage month). We have read that they are to sacrifice an animal and share the meat with the poor. Sometimes they send money for meat to poor people too far away to be receiving it directly.

- What holidays do Christians celebrate that help us remember something that happened in Bible times?
- Is there anything we do for any of those holidays that gives help to people who are poor or needy?
- How could this help us to remember to worship God and not have idols of greediness?

Update your list of things you have learned about Islam and continue to display it on a poster or with signs.

Activities (See Activities Instruction Section for details.)
- Look for a children's book about Malcolm X in the library, and read about his going on pilgrimage to Mecca. If a child has read about Malcolm in advance, ask for a report. Make a mural (or do some other project) to show what you have learned about the influence of the *hajj* on Malcolm's life and how that changed the ways many African Americans understood Islam.
- Invite the class to look at a picture of the Ka'ba. Have each child make a cube as a reminder of the Ka'ba. The directions and materials needed are found on page 228.

Study Guide

> **The Ka'ba**
>
> The Ka'ba is believed by Muslims to be the first place of worship of the One God, dating back to Adam and to Abraham.
>
> "[The Ka'ba is a] black, cube-shaped structure . . . which contains a mass of meteorite material that had been venerated as a shrine by Arabs for centuries before Muhammad. Muhammad rededicated the shrine to God; the stone within it is to Muslims a sign of God's covenant with Abraham. In a ritual called tawaf, pilgrims walk around the Ka'ba three times during the Hajj; at the beginning, after the sacrifice, and before leaving Mecca. Those who are able to be close to the stone meditate near it and kiss it; others extend their arms toward it while reciting the pilgrim's prayer."[6]

For the Next Session

Ask children to be ready for the next session, in accordance with your prepared plans. Do they need to read parts of the book at home? Do they need to bring anything? Be sure you tell parents what is needed, preferably in writing.

The next unit contains one session that can be used for all children. You will need to find a picture of a *tasbih* (a string of beads Muslim use to recite the Ninety-nine Names of God). If you work with a class of Christian and Muslim children, invite your Muslim students to bring a *tasbih*. You may also try to find a rosary or a picture of one.

Ka'ba

---

6. R. Marston Speight, *God Is One: The Way of Islam,* 2nd ed. (New York: Friendship Press, 2001), p. 43.

Unit 3
Ya'kub/Jacob

The Big Ideas
The story: Joseph
The concept: Good coming out of evil intent
The belief/practice: God is in control of all creation.

Joseph: Notes for Adults
The story of Joseph is the only extensive, uninterrupted narrative in the entire Qur'an (Surah 12). It is considered the most beautiful of stories because of Joseph's generosity and because of its lessons on how a person can be a righteous ruler without insisting on absolute power.

In the Bible, the Joseph story demonstrates God's plan to work for the good of Israel and all peoples. Joseph is presented as a reconciler who restored relationships between himself and his brothers. This restored relationship shows God's intention that their descendants—the tribes of Israel—shall overcome their strife with one another and live in peace as one people. Throughout the Hebrew Scriptures, Joseph is mentioned as the ancestor of the two major tribes of the northern kingdom, Israel. Later, in the New Testament, Joseph is remembered for his faith that God would enable his descendants to leave Egypt and take his body to be buried in Canaan (Hebrews 11:22).

Study Guide

Materials Needed
- ☐ Materials for plaques (see page 230)
- ☐ Newsprint lists from previous sessions
- ☐ Markers
- ☐ Photocopies of "Ninety-nine Names of God" (page 244) (*optional*)
- ☐ Photocopies of "The *Bismillah*" (page 243) (*optional*)
- ☐ Picture of a *tasbih* (see page 197)
- ☐ Picture of a rosary (see Activities section, page 196)

Unit 3: All Children

Preparation
This unit lends itself to an extended appreciation of its story. Plan to spend half the session on reading all or part of the material from Unit 3. Consider how to make the reading period as comfortable and interesting as possible. After reading the story, spend time in discussion, using the questions, but allow time for activity as well, as a balance to the long period of listening.

Suggested Introductory Questions
❷ What has been your favorite story so far? Why?
❷ Who can name Abraham's son? (Jacob) Can anyone name Jacob's sons?

Hearing the Stories
Read out loud "The Sons of Ya'kub/Jacob" (page 37) through the end of Unit 3.

❷ What parts of the story do you particularly like?
❷ Muslims think of Joseph as an example for how to live. What things did he do that you think would be good to follow as an example? Are there things he did that you think would not be good to follow? (Are these things told in the Bible or in the Qur'an or in both?) Who did Joseph think helped him have good behavior?
❷ What have you been taught are especially important ways to behave?
❷ What do you think is the lesson of the story of Joseph?

Many Christians believe the words at the end of the story in the Bible tell us something very important about God. Joseph says to his brothers, "You plotted evil against me, but God turned it into good. . . ." Christians and Muslims believe God is in control of the whole creation.

In conversation, give attention to God's control of our daily lives and God's control of bigger events of history.

If you will be doing the activity related to the expression *inshallah*, talk about it now. Add to your list of names/descriptions of God, if something new has emerged in this session. If you will be doing the activity related to the Ninety-nine Names of God, talk about it now.

Unit 3: Ya'kub/Jacob

Activities (See Activities Instruction Section for details.)
- Make a plaque that can be completed in the next session. For this session, decide between two possible options:

1. Have the children write *"inshallah"* or "God willing" in the center of the plaque. Before beginning work, talk about the expression. Some Christians say "God willing" as a way of saying that God is in control and that they believe God can bring good. If these Christians were in the Joseph story, they would say, "God willing, Joseph's relatives will go back home from Egypt some day."

Muslims say *"inshallah,"* meaning "God willing." Do you say this or know anyone who says this?

Inshallah is used when talking about the future, since humans do not know when or how things will happen—even ordinary things—because we do not fully control our lives. Thus, when leaving home in the morning, it is appropriate to say, *"Inshallah* I'll be home by five tonight," that is, God willing, I'll be home by five tonight.

2. Have them write one of the names of God from "Ninety-nine Names of God" (page 244) in the center of the plaque.

Before beginning the activity, pass out copies and look at a list in English of the "Ninety-nine Names of God" (page 244) to see what characteristics of God are highlighted. Allow the children to comment on names that are their favorites (particularly for Muslim children, if they are present), or that seem either expected or surprising in such a list (particularly for Christian children). Compare the Ninety-nine Names with your list of names/descriptions of God to see which names are on your list.

- You may want to show a picture of Muslim beads on a string (*tasbih*), to see how the 33 beads are used in three rounds to recite the 99 names. (These beads are often called "worry beads" in English because many Muslims have the habit of carrying them and fingering them while sitting, walking, or talking.)
  If appropriate, talk about how some Christians use a rosary, which looks very much like the Muslim beads. (The rosary used by Catholics is a string of 50 small beads divided into sections by four larger beads that is used as an aid to memory and concentration while meditating and reciting the Hail Mary and the Lord's Prayer.)

Closing

Close the session, if you wish, with the following story about how God gives gifts to us, according to God's will:

This is another story about Mullah Nasruddin. One day he saw a group of children arguing about how to divide a small pile of candies between them. "What's the trouble?" Mullah asked. "There aren't an even number of candies for all of us," one boy said, "so we can't agree about what to do. Will you help us?" Mullah agreed. But he then asked, "Do you want these divided the human way or God's way?" Thinking that they should say so, they answered that they wanted them divided God's way. After hearing this, Mullah began giving out the sweets—five to one child, two to another, seven to another, eleven to another. The children were immediately upset and yelled out, "This isn't fair!" "You said you wanted it God's way," Mullah said. "If you had asked for the human way I would have given each the same amount, but God gives in different amounts to different people. That is how God takes care of us all."

For the Next Session
Ask children to be ready for the next session, in accordance with your prepared plans. Do they need to read parts of the book at home? Do they need to bring anything? Be sure you tell parents what is needed, preferably in writing.

The next unit is about Moses. This extensive story cannot be read in full during the session. Arrange for each of the children to hear the story at home, ahead of the group meeting.

tasbih

Units 4 and 5
Musa/Moses and the Desert Journey

The Big Ideas
The story: Moses
The concept: laws as guidance
The belief/practice: the *shahada,* Muhammad as messenger of God

> **Moses: Notes for Adults**
> Moses is recognized as the liberator of the people of Israel and the lawgiver in both the Bible and the Qur'an. He is referred to in the Qur'an as *Kalim Allah,* "the word of God" (Surah 4:164), and the Bible speaks of him in superlative terms as a prophet whom God knew face to face (Deuteronomy 34:10). Moses is depicted in both scriptures not only as a great leader who possessed humility and perseverance but also as one who displayed the human qualities of anger, frustration, and lack of self-confidence.
>
> Moses is the primary figure in the biblical narrative of four of the five books comprising the Torah—in the books of Exodus, Leviticus, Numbers, and Deuteronomy. The Qur'an refers to him more than to any other prophet. Many of the events recounted in the Bible's story of Moses' life are also found in the Qur'an. In the New Testament, Moses is primarily mentioned in connection with the law, but he is also considered a model of faith (Hebrews 3:2; 11:24) as the one specially chosen by God to free his people and give them God's law.
>
> The Qur'an draws many parallels between the lives and struggles of Moses and Muhammad: both faced false charges of practicing magic and diverting their people from the faith, both were adopted sons, both went into exile, both received a revelation, and both wrestled with their own community. Muhammad is considered to have the same religion as Moses (Surah 42:13).

Muhammad: Notes for Adults

Islam considers the revelation of the Qur'an to Muhammad to be a great miracle. Muhammad, a man who may not have been literate (Surah 7:157), orally received the recitation in Arabic over a period of 23 years from the angel Jabra'il/Gabriel. He repeated what he received to his followers, who wrote it down and collected it into a book, the Qur'an (the "recitation").

Muhammad is only named four times in the Qur'an. He is called a Messenger (*rasul*) (Surah 48:29), but he is only a Messenger (Surah 3:144). He is also called the "Seal of the Prophets" (Surah 33:40), meaning that he was the last Prophet (*nabi*) because all that one must know about God and about how one is to act is in the Qur'an. The truth was revealed to Muhammad and is to be believed and followed (Surah 47:2). Like the prophets before him, Muhammad told people they should worship only God and warned people they should not worship other gods.

Muhammad lived at the end of the sixth century and the first part of the seventh century of the Common Era. He was an orphan (Surah 93:6–8) who was raised by his grandfather and then his uncle in Mecca. As a young man, he worked for a rich merchant's widow, Khadija, as a trader and married her; all Muhammad's children but one—including his daughter Fatima—were born to her and she was his first follower.

Muhammad began to receive revelations from God when he was about forty. About ten years later he and his followers moved to Yathrib (which we know as Medina) at the invitation of some followers there, in order to escape the pressures from unbelievers in Mecca. In Medina he became the leader of the emerging Muslim community. The Muslim calendar is dated from the time of the migration to Medina (the *hijra*); the year 622 C.E., in the solar calendar used in the West today, is the first year in the Islamic lunar calendar.

After Khadija's death and during the last years of his life, Muhammad married a number of women. Among these wives was 'A'isha, who contributed to the record of his life. The early believers preserved the sayings and deeds of Muhammad (*hadith*) and they are examples for the life and practice of Muslims.

Units 4 and 5: Musa/Moses and the Desert Journey

Unit 4/5-A: Muslim and Christian Children Together

Islamic laws and standards

"[Islam is] a complete system and way of life which embraces the entirety of the human being's existence. . . . [T]here is no fragmentation or division within the personality of the Muslim due to the splitting of life into compartments or applying different rules or criteria to different parts of life. The same divine system, the same God-given laws and standards govern all aspects of life, and all of an individual's actions are considered by Islam as worship in the broadest sense of the term if they are done with the sincere intention of pleasing God in keeping His injunctions.

"[Islam] is clear and specific about matters which are prohibited . . . as well as about those that are obligatory . . . The guide for the Muslim's conduct in all spheres of his life is, first, the Holy Qur'an and, second, the Prophet's example or practice . . ."[7]

Materials Needed
- Newsprint
- Markers
- Plaques from previous unit
- Materials to work on plaques (see page 231)
- Photocopies of "Geometric Patterns" (pages 245–247)
- Crayons, colored pencils, watercolors and brushes, or markers
- Scissors (*optional*)
- Tape (*optional*)
- Large sheets of paper or light cardboard (*optional*)
- Large construction paper

Preparation
Allot two-thirds or more of your session time for discussion. Read selected parts of "In the Desert of Sinai" through "The Commandments," then "Back into the Desert"; summarize unread parts sufficiently to make the story hang together. To provide the foundation for the discussion, be sure to read about idolatry, the giving of the law/commandments, and the Lord telling Moses to write a song.

Suggested Introductory Questions

❷ In Jesus' day, his people followed the "law of Moses." They asked Jesus which law was the greatest. What did he answer? Which of the Ten Commandments is nearest to this? What else did Jesus say was like that law? (Matthew 22:36–40; cf. Unit 8, "'Isa/Jesus and His Disciples"). You may wish to write Jesus' summary of the law on a board or newsprint, so that all the children may see it.

---

7. Suzanne Haneef, *What Everyone Should Know about Islam and Muslims* (Chicago: Kazi Publications, 1996), p. 100.

- Do Christians today follow the Ten Commandments? The Great Commandment and Jesus' summary of the law? Talk about the ways Christians do this.
- Do Muslims have laws that guide them? What things do Muslim families do because they are guided by Islamic law?

The children's varying answers may highlight the specificity of Muslim standards and the more general guidance Christians take from their scripture and teachings. Both Muslims and Christians declare that they seek to please God by following the way they have been taught by God to live. In your discussion, do not dwell on reward systems (human or divine) that may be connected to obedience or disobedience of God's laws.

Hearing the Stories
Read out loud selected parts from "In the Desert of Sinai" through "The Commandments." Finish by reading out loud "Back into the Desert." Make sure to summarize the unread parts to make the story hang together.

- Moses/Musa, his brother Aaron/Harun, and his sister Miriam/Maryam are all called prophets of God in Christian tradition. We have talked about Noah/Nuh as a prophet warning the people. About what did Moses, and his sister and brother, need to warn the Israelites?
- Recall stories heard in earlier sessions about people who followed idols.
- Muhammad was given a message that Moses/Musa was not only a "prophet" (*nabi*) but also a "messenger" (*rasul*). A messenger is given a message from God for a book. What book(s) contain the message of Moses? Muhammad is also called both a "prophet" and a "messenger." What book contains the message given to Muhammad?

You may wish to go back to read again from Unit 2, "The Sons of Ibrahim/Abraham," page 31, beginning "All these messages were written down in a book . . ."

- When we talked about the call to prayer, we looked at the words "There is no god except God." These words are followed by the words "Muhammad is the messenger of God" (Surah 48:29). All Muslims say these words in what is called the *shahada:* "I witness that there is no god except God and that Muhammad is the messenger of God." What are some of the occasions on which Muslims say this?
- In the *shahada*, Muslims say what all Muslims believe. Are there words Christians use to tell what they believe? What are they? (Accept from the Christian children any answer that concentrates on belief, with preference toward formulations used in the rites of worship, e.g., the Nicene or the Apostles' Creed. Depending on their experience, children may also mention a catechism, a particular Bible verse, even the words of a particular hymn.)

Units 4 and 5: Musa/Moses and the Desert Journey

❷ Muhammad and Moses were alike in many ways. In what ways were they alike?

Help the children recognize that both Moses and Muhammad received revelations and that these provided the basis for law/guidance about how to live (Surah 28:43ff.). They may also offer other suggestions that are valid.

Activities (See Activities Instruction Section for details.)
- If you worked on plaques during the previous session, complete this work by making geometric borders for them (see page 231).
  The geometric patterns used within Islamic art are an expression of the value given to the consistency of God's law by Muslims. You may wish to talk about this with older children.
- Have the children create more geometric borders using the information on page 232).
- Have the children make posters of the words "You shall love the Lord your God with all your heart and your neighbor as yourself" or of the words of the *shahada*.

Closing
Finish with a prayer thanking the Lord for guidance and mercy.

For the Next Session
Ask children to be ready for the next session, in accordance with your prepared plans. Do they need to read parts of the book at home? Do they need to bring anything? Be sure you tell parents what is needed, preferably in writing.

Study Guide

Materials Needed
- Bible (*optional*)
- Newsprint lists from previous sessions
- Markers
- Plaques from previous unit
- Materials to work on plaques (see page 231)
- Photocopies of "Geometric Patterns" (pages 245–247)
- Crayons, colored pencils, watercolors and brushes, or markers
- Scissors (*optional*)
- Tape (*optional*)
- Large construction paper
- Felt-tipped markers

Units 4/5-B: Christian Children

Preparation
Allot two-thirds or more of your session time for discussion. Read selected parts of "In the Desert of Sinai" through "The Commandments," then "Back into the Desert"; summarize unread parts sufficiently to make the story hang together. To provide the foundation for the discussion, be sure to read about idolatry, the giving of the law/commandments, and the Lord telling Moses to write a song.

Suggested Introductory Questions
Begin by remembering the story of Joseph and what you discussed at the end of the story: God is in control of all that God created and works to bring good things even out of hardship and evil. As a way of remembering this, some Christians say "God willing" and Muslims say *"inshallah."* If God wants us to live good lives, will God not guide us in what we are to do?

❷ Muslims talk about "the straight path" that God shows us (Surah 1:6). What do you think of when you hear about God showing us a straight path? Note that Jeremiah 31:9 uses the same vocabulary, saying that God will "let them walk . . . in a straight path in which they will not stumble."

Christians read from Psalm 1 about people being happy who do not follow "the path of sinners" but who follow the law of God. (Depending on the time available and the age of your group, you may want to read the psalm.)

❷ How would laws help us to go in a straight way? We are going to read today about Moses, who was given laws by God as guidance for the people he was leading.

Hearing the Stories
Read the selected parts of "In the Desert of Sinai" through "The Commandments," and finish by reading "Back into the Desert." Summarize the unread parts so the story hangs together. After you have finished reading, remind the children that the Commandments given to Moses still are important guides for both Jews and Christians, and God also gave Moses other laws.

❷ Have you been taught to follow some or all of the Ten Commandments? What did Jesus say was the most important law? Which of the Ten Commandments is nearest to this? What did Jesus say was the second most important law? (Matthew 22:36–40.) How do you and your family try to follow these things that Jesus taught?

Tell the children that Muslims also give great importance to laws about how to live. If you did not read the section called "The Commandments," read out loud the section from the Qur'an where the Qur'an tells about the laws given to Moses (page 89).

❷ Why do you think the laws can be called "a guidance and a mercy" (Surah 7:145, 154)? What is mercy? Why did Moses' people need mercy?
❷ The Qur'an says that God guided Moses and Aaron to the "straight way" and that God gave them a book that helps make things clear (Surah 37:114–118). It says that Moses/Musa was both a "prophet" (*nabi*) and a "messenger" (*rasul*). A messenger is given a message from God for a book. What books of the Bible contain the message of Moses? The Qur'an calls these books the Tawrat. (Jews call them the Torah.) What book contains the message given to Muhammad as a messenger of God?

When we talked about the call to prayer, we learned the words "There is no god except God." These words are followed by the words "and Muhammad is the messenger of God" (Surah 48:29). All Muslims say these words in what is called the *shahada*: "I witness that there is no god except God and that Muhammad is the messenger of God." These words are said frequently. They are whispered in the ear of a newborn baby who is a Muslim from birth. They are said by someone who was not born a Muslim and becomes one. They are said in the mosque.

❷ In the *shahada*, Muslims say what all Muslims believe. Are there words Christians use to tell what they believe? What are they?

You may want to talk briefly about the Apostles' Creed, the Brief Statement of Faith of the Presbyterian Church (U.S.A.), or some other statement of faith. Children may also mention some specific passage of the Bible or some generally used set of words they have heard.

The Qur'an says that Muhammad, like Moses, gave people a message of how God wants people to live. Laws guide people in doing this (Surah 28:43ff.). Muslims follow laws today based on the Qur'an and on the way Muhammad lived (found in the *hadith*, the traditional reports of Muhammad's deeds and sayings). These laws are very practical and specific.

Say: "We have learned that all Muslims say the *shahada:* 'I witness that there is no god except God and that Muhammad is God's prophet.'" Note if this is on the newsprint list about what the children have learned about Islam. If not, make sure to write it in.

Say: "We have learned that all Muslims who are financially and physically able are required to go to Mecca on pilgrimage at least once in their lives." Likewise, note if this is on the list about what they have learned about Islam.

Share that they will learn about the following:

- We will learn that there are definite times in each day when Muslims are to pray.
- We will learn that Muslims are required to give a certain amount of their wealth to help the poor and needy.
- We will learn that during one month of the year Muslims are required to fast.

There are many other set patterns for living that are followed by Muslims. For example, we have talked about dressing modestly; there are certain things that Muslims do not eat (such as pork) or drink (alcoholic drinks).

A Society Consistent with God's Will

"The goal . . . beyond simple obedience and personal edification is the establishment of a society on earth which is consistent with God's will, as articulated in the Qur'an and traditions of the Prophet [Muhammad]. It is these sources and their interpretation by subsequent generations of scholars that form the basis of Islamic law, called *shari'ah.*"[8]

❷ Christians are taught that when we love God, we show it by obeying God (John 14:15, 21). What do you think are the things we must do to obey God?

❷ Are there things that you do because you are a Christian? (Help the children think about defining characteristics of themselves as Christians and the source of this in the teaching of the church; for example, attending church worship regularly may derive from "keep the Sabbath day holy," or the intention of living according to the commandment "love your neighbor as yourself" may lead to behaviors that seek to be loving in every circumstance.)

Activities
Use the suggestions under Unit 4/5-A on page 202.

---

8. *Christians and Muslims in Dialogue: Facets of a Relationship* (Louisville, KY: Worldwide Ministries Division, Presbyterian Church (U.S.A.), 2002), p. 27.

Closing
Finish with a prayer thanking the Lord for guidance and mercy.

For the Next Session
Ask children to be ready for the next session, in accordance with your prepared plans. Do they need to read parts of the book at home? Do they need to bring anything? Be sure you tell parents what is needed, preferably in writing.

Read the section under Room Arrangement for Unit 6 for instructions on selecting the stories to read. If you choose to make the reed pens, make sure you have several adult volunteers to assist in this activity.

Unit 6
Guides, Judges, and Kings

The Big Ideas
The stories: David, Solomon
The concept: God as king
The belief/practice: ritual worship/prayer

The plans for this unit will call for a reading of Psalm 103, found on page 248. The parts in bold type are to be read in unison by all the children. The other parts can be read by older children or by one or more adults. Read in formal style, as you would use in formal worship.

> **David and Solomon: Notes for Adults**
> David is portrayed in the Bible as a model king. The Qur'an says David was a representative of God (*khalifa*) who judged with justice (Surah 38:26). David was a religious man who had a special relationship with God; when David sinned, he repented to God for what he had done.
>
> Only a few incidents in the life of David are recounted in the Qur'an but many are found in Islamic folktales—how he killed Goliath, that he married Saul's daughter and shared Saul's authority, that Saul became jealous of him, that he hid from Saul in a cave and was protected by a spider web over the entrance, that he had an affair with Bathsheba, and that he planned to build the Temple.
>
> In both the Bible and the Qur'an, David is recognized as having musical gifts and being the writer of Psalms, one of the three parts of the Bible referred to in the Qur'an (as *Zabur*). The Qur'an says it was a gift from God that the mountains and birds would sing praise to God with David (Surah 34:10). One verse of a psalm from the Bible (Psalm 37:29) is repeated in the Qur'an (Surah 21:105; cf. the psalm quotation by Jesus in Matthew 5:3).
>
> The biblical account of David presents him as a man of honor who has the gifts of a diplomat, a warrior, and a politician. Biblically, he is also portrayed as a father who struggles with his ambitious sons. The Qur'an

emphasizes that David, along with his son Solomon, had the gift of wisdom and that together they decide a difficult case (Surah 21:78). David is also credited with inventing how to make coats of mail from iron (Surah 21:80; 34:11).

In later biblical writings, David and his kingdom have significance that today's theologians describe as "eschatological": the future kingdom will be an ideal one with the Messiah, a descendant of David, as king. Jesus is a descendent of David and the inaugurator of the messianic kingdom.

David's son Solomon is said in the Qur'an to know the speech of birds and animals (Surah 27:16) and to have amazing powers over the forces of nature (Surah 38:36). He had such a great love for horses that one time this caused him to forget to do his evening prayers. He repented, was forgiven, and was given more powers from God (Surah 38:30–40).

Study Guide

Materials Needed
- ☐ Photocopies of "Psalm 103" (page 248)
- ☐ Dictionary
- ☐ A prayer rug
- ☐ A Qur'an stand
- ☐ Hymnals or Psalters
- ☐ Materials to make reed pens (see pages 233–234)
- ☐ Photocopies of "The *Bismillah*" (page 243)
- ☐ Bottles of India ink (*optional*)
- ☐ Calligraphy makers (*optional*)

Unit 6-A: Muslim and Christian Children Together

Preparation
Select the portions of Unit 6 you will read, depending on the time available and the interests of the children. Be sure to read about David writing psalms and Solomon building the temple. Encourage reading of the entire unit's stories at home, as possible.

Suggested Introductory Questions
Pass out copies of "Psalm 103" (page 248), and invite the children to join you in reading it. Point out that the psalm comes from the Bible and is a kind of prayer. David wrote down many songs, known as psalms.

- What are the big ideas in the psalm (in bold type, repeated)? In the psalm, who praises God? For what things do they praise God? How can creation praise God?

Hearing the Stories
Read out loud the selected stories for Unit 6.

- David was a man who praised and worshiped God, but he also made mistakes. What do the stories in *Abraham and Ibrahim* tell us about David's mistakes?
- How does Psalm 103 say God treats sinners? What can you remember from stories we have read in earlier sessions about how God has treated sinners?
- Christians sometimes use psalms in the rituals of worship. What is a ritual? (Look up the word in a dictionary, if necessary.) Many Christian churches read psalms every time they worship on Sunday. Many Christians read psalms as prayers when they are alone. Many of the psalms have been translated in ways that can be sung with music. When do you use psalms, if you do? When do others in your family use them?
- Muslims have rituals of prayer (*salat*) that are part of their daily lives. Friday is the day for praying together at noon in the mosque. Where do the people in your family do prayers? What is done before prayers, to prepare for them? Can you describe what is done during the prayers themselves? How is the Qur'an used in the prayers? (The first surah of the Qur'an is repeated two to four times in every prayer, and other verses are also said.)

There is potential vocabulary confusion between the two Arabic words translated into English as "prayer." The prescribed ritual (*salat*) is most commonly described as prayer in Muslim discussion. But Christians identify with a freer form of supplication and praise (*dua*) that is also practiced by Muslims.

- Muslims pray five times every day, at set times. They are reminded of God throughout the day in this special way. Is there anything special that reminds Christians of God every day, during the day?
- David wanted to build a temple but it was his son Solomon who was able to build it. Why did God not allow David to build it?
- To what kind of building does your family go for worship with others? Tell about the building and the special places in the building. What do the people face as they pray or worship? Is there a special place used by the preacher? What is the place where you belong in the building?

When worshipers face the *mihrab*, or niche, in a mosque, they are facing toward Mecca, the direction in which all Muslims around the world face when they pray; a pulpit, the *minbar*, is the place from which the sermon is preached. Christians sit in pews in most churches, facing the front of the sanctuary, where there is usually a pulpit, a Bible, the cross, a communion table.

- How do you show respect for the things you use in worship that are especially important? For example, how do you treat the Qur'an? The Bible? Do you remove your shoes when you enter the place of worship? Do you wear certain kinds of clothes when you go to church? To the mosque? Do you wear certain kinds of clothes when you pray at home? Do you wash in special ways before prayer or worship? Are you free to talk while worship is going on in the mosque? In the church?
- Do you feel something special when you are worshiping or praying with many other people in the church or in the mosque? What happens when someone who doesn't know what to do comes to your church or mosque? How do you welcome new people?

Prayers
Muslims pray five times each day, at dawn, noon, afternoon, sunset, and night. Ritual washing (*wudu*) precedes the prayers, which are performed on a rug. Recitation from the Qur'an is part of each prayer. Worshipers stand, bow, touch the ground with their foreheads, and sit. Prayers are said alone or with others—at home, at work, while traveling, in the mosque. In the mosque, worshipers stand shoulder to shoulder as they pray—men in the front and women behind or in another room. Small children may accompany a parent.

"Performing [the prayers] regularly serves as a repeated reminder to the Muslim during the day and night of his relationship with his Creator and his place in the total scheme of Reality. Its purpose is to keep him from ever forgetting that he belongs, not to himself or even to the people who are closest to him, but to God, and that he is His servant, obedient to His command."[9]

Activities (See Activities Instruction Section for details.)
- Arrange ahead to have some items available for showing to the group, such as a prayer rug, a Qur'an stand, a hymnbook, or a Psalter. Collect some pictures, as well, that will show things that cannot be brought, such as a pulpit, a *mihrab* (showing the direction to face for prayer). Spend time looking at items you have brought. Talk about them together.
- Make a reed pen used in writing Arabic script (see pages 233–234).
- If there is time, have the children practice writing the *Bismillah* with the reed pen or a calligraphy marker (see page 234).
- Learn to sing one of the psalms arranged with music, as found in a Christian hymnal. (After consultation between the Muslim and Christian planners, you may decide that Christian children will do this activity and will share what they have learned with the Muslim children.)
- Visit a mosque and/or church to look at special features of the building and talk about how the building is used in worship.

Closing
Read Psalm 103 again as your closing prayer.

For the Next Session
Ask children to be ready for the next session, in accordance with your prepared plans. Do they need to read parts of the book at home? Do they need to bring anything? Be sure you tell parents what is needed, preferably in writing.

---

9. Suzanne Haneef, *What Everyone Should Know about Islam and Muslims* (Chicago: Kazi Publications, 1996), p. 52.

Unit 6: Guides, Judges, and Kings

Materials Needed
- Photocopies of "Psalm 103" (page 248)
- Dictionary
- Prayer rug (or a picture)
- Qur'an stand (or a picture)
- Materials to create reed pens (see pages 233–234)
- Photocopies of "The *Bismillah*" (page 243)
- Bottles of India ink (*optional*)
- Calligraphy makers (*optional*)
- Hymnals

Unit 6-B: Christian Children

Preparation
If it is possible for children to read or be read to at home, arrange for a reading of the entire unit there. Use brief segments when you are together, to serve as reminders and to facilitate the discussion.

Suggested Introductory Questions
We are going to talk about David today. Let's think about the different things David was, and then let's use our imaginations to think about what it would be like to be in those positions.

Hearing the Stories
Read the selected segments from Unit 6 out loud. Make sure to share portions that correspond with the discussion questions.

- David was a young shepherd. What did our story tell us about how he was treated as a shepherd? Did his father think of him as an important person who should be noticed by others?
- David became the king. Was he an important enough person to be able to do whatever he wanted? What parts of the story would give you this idea? How do you imagine other people treat a king? What do you imagine people do when they go to see a king who is treated as a very important person? Would they bow down, for example?
- David was also a writer of psalms. Some of the psalms say that God is "king." David knew how a king is treated. How do you think he believed humans should respond to God, the king? Would this include obeying God? The story showed that David did not always obey God. How? This can be called "sin."

Pass out copies and as a group read "Psalm 103" (page 248). Point out that this psalm is a kind of prayer.

- What are the big ideas in the psalm (bold type, repeated words/phrases)? For what things is God praised? How can creation praise God?

❓ How does the psalm say God treats sinners? What can you remember from stories we have read in earlier sessions about how God has treated sinners in those stories?

❓ Christians use psalms in the rituals of worship. What is a ritual? (Look up the word in a dictionary, if necessary.) Many Christian churches read psalms every Sunday. Many Christians read psalms as prayers when they are alone. Many of the psalms have been translated in ways that can be sung with music, as hymns. When do you use psalms, if you do? When do others in your family use them?

Muslims have rituals of prayer (*salat*). They are told to pray five times every day, at set times. Friday is the day for praying together at noon in the mosque. When Muslims pray, there are not only special words to be said (including the *shahada* and readings from the Qur'an), there are also special ways of standing, bowing, putting the forehead on the ground, and sitting. These positions may remind us of the very special respect that is shown to a king. They are signs of submission to God. Remember that we have said that "Muslim" means a person who "submits."

Show pictures of the postures of prayer.

❓ Muslims' prayers remind them of God many times a day in a special way. Is there anything that reminds Christians of God every day, during the day?

> Two Arabic words are translated as prayer: first, the prescribed ritual prayers (*salat*) and, second, a freer form of supplication and praise (*dua*) more akin to what Christians think of when they hear the word "prayer."

❓ David wanted to build a temple but it was his son Solomon who was able to build it. Why did God not allow David to build it?
❓ To what kind of building does your family go for worship with others? Talk about the building and the special places in the building. For instance, is there a special place used by the preacher?

A mosque, used by Muslims, has special places in it. The worshipers sit on the floor on rugs. They face toward a place in the room marked to show the direction the people are to face when they pray. Muslims all over the world face toward Mecca when they pray. Wherever a mosque is, the direction of

Mecca is marked. There is also a special place for the preacher to sit as he delivers the sermon.

❷ How do you show respect for the things you use in worship that are especially important? For example, how do you treat the Bible at home and at church? Muslims treat the Qur'an very carefully, not putting it on the floor or under other books in a stack. Do you remove your shoes when you enter your place of worship? Muslims do, when they enter a mosque; Christians in some countries do, when they enter the church. Do you wear certain kinds of clothes when you go to church? Muslim women cover their heads when they pray, even if they do not do so at other times; some Christian women also cover their heads. Do you wash in special ways before going to church? This is something Muslims do before they pray; there is a place in the mosque for washing.

❷ When Muslims pray, they stand shoulder to shoulder in a line. This is a special time of feeling that all the people are one group—all made by God, the Creator, and all worshiping God together. What, if anything, makes you feel like you belong when you are in your church? Do you feel that you belong to the same Christian community with Christians in other parts of the world? Why?

Activities (See Activities Instruction Section for details.)
- Arrange ahead to have some articles used by Muslims to show the group, such as a prayer rug or a Qur'an stand (or pictures of these).
- Use the suggestions in Unit 6-A.

Closing
Arrange some brief act of worship to use as you close the session—reading a psalm, singing a hymn, saying a prayer, and so on. If possible, include the themes of God's forgiveness of sin, and our praise and thanks to God for God's creation and for God's kindness.

For the Next Session
Ask children to be ready for the next session, in accordance with your prepared plans. Do they need to read parts of the book at home? Do they need to bring anything? Be sure you tell parents what is needed, preferably in writing.

The next session covers all of Unit 7 and the first section of Unit 8, titled "The Child 'Isa/Jesus" (the Qur'anic account of Jesus' birth but not the biblical account). Make a selection that can be read in one-third of your session time; summarize what you cannot read. You will also need to decide whether or not to serve Middle Eastern food (including dates). Check with parents to see if any of the children have food allergies you need to be aware of.

Unit 7
The Births of Jesus/'Isa and John/Yahya

The Big Ideas
The stories: the births of John the Baptist and Jesus
The concept: God as giver of life
The beliefs/practices: angels, fasting

Unit 7: All Children

Materials Needed
- ❑ Newsprint lists from previous units
- ❑ Markers
- ❑ Tablecloth
- ❑ Middle Eastern food (see pages 235–236)
- ❑ Serving dishes, paper plates and cup, tableware, as needed

Preparation
This session covers all of Unit 7 and the first section of Unit 8, titled "The Child 'Isa/Jesus" (the Qur'anic account of Jesus' birth but not the biblical account). Make a selection that can be read in one-third of your session time and summarize what you cannot read.

Suggested Introduction
The stories in the Bible and in the Qur'an are told quite differently. Let's look at them and remember other stories we have heard earlier. Provide assistance, as needed, for the children to recall and make connections that may seem difficult.

> **Fasting: Notes for Adults**
> "Fasting makes the Muslim disciplined, steadfast and resilient like a soldier who forgoes or postpones the satisfaction of his normal needs at the order of his Commander. . . . Fasting also enables the Muslim to feel

Unit 7: The Births of Jesus/'Isa and John/Yahya

> with the poor who daily experience hunger and to be active in compassion and charity toward them.
>
> "Islam recognizes that physical needs and appetites, particularly those of food, drink and sex, are powerful factors in human life, tying the human being to dependence on and preoccupation with his bodily needs and desires. Hence the Muslim is asked for one month out of the year [the month of Ramadan] to do without the satisfaction of these needs by day in order to develop his spiritual nature. . . . Ramadan is thus a month . . . during which the Muslim . . . has a unique opportunity . . . to devote himself to God and to his spiritual development."[10]

Hearing the Stories

Read out loud the selected passages from Unit 7 and the first section of Unit 8, titled "The Child 'Isa/Jesus." Depending on the age and attention span of your children, you may wish to read a segment and discuss it before going on to the next segment.

- In these stories, angels appear to announce that special babies will be born. Why do you think it is angels that bring the messages? Why do you think Zechariah and Mary were afraid when an angel came? To whom else do you remember an angel appearing?

Angels, according to Islamic belief, are agents of God who do God's will as messengers. They are created from light, and though they are intelligent beings, they do not have free will. The angel Gabriel/Jabra'il, who makes announcements to both Zechariah and Mary in the Bible, is the angel identified by Muhammad as having recited the Qur'an to him.

- Elizabeth was old and had no children. Zechariah and Elizabeth were surprised that she was going to have a baby. What does it mean, in the Qur'an, when God says, "[This] is easy for Me. I created you before, from nothing!" What other story have we read in which the mother was surprised when she was very old and had a baby son? (Genesis 18:12–14, Surah 11:72)
- Mary had no husband, and no man had made her pregnant. What do you think it means, in the Qur'an, when she is shown a bird made out of clay that becomes a living bird when God breathes on it? Do you know a Bible story in which God breathes on the shape of a man God has made from dust and it becomes a living person? (Genesis 2:27)
- The Qur'an also says the angel told Mary, "The Lord but says, 'Be,' and it is." When, in the Bible, did God say that something should be made and it is made? (Genesis 1:3ff., Surah 2:117)

10. Suzanne Haneef, *What Everyone Should Know about Islam and Muslims* (Chicago: Kazi Publications, 1996), p. 57.

For adult reflection, see the box in Unit 8, "Jesus: Notes for Adults" (page 220), concerning Jesus as "the last Adam."

> In the section "Mary/Maryam," Mary is told, "[Your son] will be called the Son of the Most High, and the Lord God will give him the throne of David" (page 139). Jesus is considered to be from the house of David, to whom God promised continuing rule (cf. Jeremiah 33:20–21). "Most High" is a frequent biblical title for God, in the psalms in particular. See the box on "Family Terms in the Bible" (page 219) for an interpretation of the Son terminology. It is recommended that, given the complex nature of this term, it not be raised as a subject for discussion with the children.

- In what way did Mary show that she was willing to do what God wanted? We call this "doing God's will." What Islamic saying did we talk about earlier that means "God willing" or "if God so wants"?
- The story of Jesus' birth in the Qur'an shows that it was a difficult time for Maryam. In what ways? What hard thing has happened in your life, when you had to choose whether or not to do what God wanted you to do?
- The Qur'an's story of Jesus' birth says that Maryam had vowed to fast. What is fasting (*sawm*)? (One ordinary English word includes "fast" in it: we eat "breakfast" after a long time of not eating overnight and so we "break the fast.") Why do you think Maryam would fast?
- Muslims fast together during the same month each year, the month of Ramadan. They do not eat or drink from dawn to sunset. This is something that all Muslims do except the ones who have reasons for not fasting—such as children, sick people, travelers, and others whose bodies, for different reasons, need food and drink during the day as well as at night. What opportunity does fasting give to Muslims? Some Christians also practice fasting. Jesus told his people that if they fasted, they should not try to get others to notice them; it should be God who knows what a person does (Matthew 6:17–18).

When Muslims fast, they also are thinking about God and are expected, in addition to not eating and drinking during daylight, to think of God, to read the Qur'an, and to follow proper behavior. When Muslims "break the fast" with what is called *iftar*, there is happiness and special food.

> **Mary and John the Baptist: Notes for Adults**
> Mary has a distinctive place in both the Bible and the Qur'an. She is portrayed in both as a pious and pure virgin chosen by God to be the mother of Jesus. It is Mary's purity as a virgin that is emphasized in the Qur'an. It is her role as a faithful mother that is important in the New Testament: she trains her son in the religious traditions of her people; she is loyal to him even when he is persecuted; and she is among those who put their faith in him after his ascension.

Mary is not venerated in the Bible; in fact, Jesus warns against such thinking (Luke 11:27–28). Rather, she is honored as a servant of God (Luke 1:38).

Mary is mentioned throughout the Qur'an, and her story is given in a Surah titled with her name (Surah 19). She, along with Jesus, is considered a sign from God (Surah 23:50) but is explicitly said not to have been divine (Surah 5:116). Mary continued to be honored in Islamic tradition.

Mary's cousin Elizabeth is reported by the Gospels to be the mother of John the Baptist, who was born shortly before Jesus. John is an important prophet in both the Bible and the Qur'an. He is particularly considered by the New Testament to be the forerunner of Jesus, while in the Qur'an he is a prophet who proclaimed the word of God (Surah 3:39).

According to the Gospels, John had an effective and successful ministry distinct from that of Jesus: He appeared from the desert, calling on his people to repent of their sins to prepare for the coming of the kingdom of God. He baptized many people, including Jesus, as a sign of their repentance. In the rest of the New Testament, John is remembered as the one who baptized for the repentance of sins and as the one who baptized Jesus.

The Qur'an does not mention the baptisms of John nor does the Qur'anic name Yahya include any reference to him as a baptizer. Rather, the Qur'an speaks of the miraculous events related to his birth, his consideration toward his parents, the wisdom he had from childhood, and his compassionate nature (Surah 19:1–15). There is a tomb in a mosque in Damascus known as that of John.

Activities (See Activities Instruction Section for details.)
- For groups of Christian children: Quickly update your posters or signs about what you have learned about Islam.
- Imagine that you are sharing an *iftar*, a meal at the time the fast is completed for the day. Prepare special foods that can be shared (see "Prepare Food to Eat Together," pages 235–236). The children might help make some typical Middle Eastern dishes. While they are in process, serve each person a few dates and a glass of water as the first things they will eat after the fast. When the food is ready, spread a tablecloth on the floor. Take off your shoes and put them in a row somewhere at the edge of the room, go to sit around the edge of the tablecloth, and enjoy the food together.

If you are in a mixed Muslim-Christian group, spend time during the meal hearing Muslims' stories about fasting. Christians might also want to tell stories about what they do during Lent, a traditional time for Christian fasting—whether they fast and, if not, whether they "give up" something for Lent as a replacement for fasting.

Closing
Close by giving thanks to God/Allah for the food you just ate.

For the Next Session
Ask children to be ready for the next session, in accordance with your prepared plans for the next session. Do they need to read parts of the book at home? Do they need to bring anything? Be sure you tell parents what is needed, preferably in writing.

Arrange for children to hear the whole Unit 8 read at home. Time will likely not allow the whole to be read during the group time. It is suggested that a teacher or parent read, segment by segment, those parts of the unit needed for children to respond to each set of questions.

Unit 8 includes an activity to work on a project to meet a local or national need that is not tied to any one religious community. Find such an organization, and begin planning for the project. See Activities section in Unit 8 for more information.

> **Family Terms in the Bible: Notes for Adults**
> Family terms for God and for relationships with God are common in the Hebrew Scriptures and were known to Jesus and his disciples/helpers and to the early church. These terms, as found in the New Testament, are relational and do not have any physical or biological meaning.
>
> The term "Father" is used to indicate "the relationship of God to all people as their Creator, who loves and cares for them (Luke 12:29–31)."
>
> "In Hebrew the expression 'son(s) of' in such phrases as 'son of peace,' 'son of consolation,' or 'sons of thunder' means 'one who has the qualities or nature of.' 'Sons of God' is used in the [Hebrew Scriptures] to indicate that the people of God are to have the qualities of God in their lives. The children of Israel were considered to be the children of God, not in a physical sense, but as a result of God's bringing the people into being by saving their ancestors from slavery (see Deuteronomy 14:1; Hosea 1:10; 11:1). 'Son of God' is also used in the [Hebrew Scriptures] to refer to the king of Israel, who was to have the quality of God by ruling with justice (2 Samuel 7:8–17; Psalms 2:6–11; 89:20–37). The kings were considered to be representative of the children of Israel. The kings had a special relationship with God who guided them in their role as kings. Jesus as a king in the line of David is also considered a son of God."[11]

---

11. Glossary, *The Holy Gospel, Study Edition* (Brisbane, Australia: United Bible Societies, 2001), pp. 914, 920–921.

Unit 8
'Isa/Jesus

The Big Ideas
The story: Jesus
The concept: service
The belief/practice: judgment, alms giving

Jesus: Notes for Adults
In the Qur'an Jesus is one of the prophets, though essentially different from all others: He was born of a virgin; had miraculous powers, including the power to raise the dead to life; and was led by the spirit of God. Jesus—both a prophet (*nabi*) and a messenger (*rasul*) from God to the people of Israel—was given a "book," the Gospel (*Injil*). He was a servant of God, a sign for humanity, and a mercy from God (Surah 19:21–30).

Biblically, Jesus is the central figure of the New Testament. His life, death, and resurrection are seen as God's provision of salvation for sinful humanity. It is only by God's free gift of undeserved grace that humans are reconciled with God. By faith and trust in Jesus as Lord and Savior, persons can come into a new relationship with God and know God's love, presence, and guidance in their lives. The accounts of Jesus' life and teaching in the Gospels are the basis for knowing how to live as God's people and for understanding how Jesus made it possible for people to know the forgiveness and love of God. In Christian tradition, Jesus is given the titles of "prophet," "priest," and "king," yet he is seen as more than a prophet in the New Testament: he is the eternal Word of God who became human to make God known. He is also called "the last Adam," a man of heaven; this man remained obedient to God and, just as we bear the image of the first Adam, we may also by faith bear the image of this latter Adam (1 Corinthians 15:45–49).

The Qur'an is understood by Muslims to deny that Jesus was crucified and resurrected from the dead; the Qur'an clearly affirms that he was taken by God into heaven (Surah 4:157–159). Further, Surah 43:61 refers to the second coming of Jesus when he will kill the Antichrist, after which there will be forty years of universal peace and security. The Qur'an explicitly denies that Jesus was divine and implies that he should not be worshiped (Surah 4:171). Jesus continues in Islam to be the example of absolute poverty and complete obedience as a servant of God.

Study Guide

> **Materials Needed**
> ❑ Information on service project (see Activities section, page 222)

Unit 8: All Children

Preparation
Some of the material in the unit deals with the most vexing questions that arise between Christians and Muslims. It is suggested that adults reread the guidelines in the Introduction and the note at the beginning of Unit 7 before they work with children on the unit.

Arrange for children to hear the whole unit read on home. It is suggested that you read out loud those parts of the unit needed for the children to respond to the questions.

Suggested Introduction
Ask the children to think of something they did this week to help others. How did helping that person make them feel? Then ask them to share what someone did to help them. How do they feel when someone helps them?

Hearing the Stories
Read out loud those parts of the unit needed for children to respond to each set of questions below.

- When John the Baptizer told people, "Prepare the way of the Lord, make his paths straight," they asked what they should do. He told them they could not escape punishment just by saying they came from Abraham's family. What did he want them to do?
- People also asked Jesus what they should do. They asked him which commandment was the most important. What did Jesus tell them when he was asked this question? Do you think that the way we treat other people is related to the way we love God? Why?
- Jesus not only showed God's love by helping those who were sick, hungry, and needy. He also asked his followers to help others who need help. What do you remember he said about this?
- What does the Qur'an say about alms giving (*zakat*)—that is, giving for the poor and needy?
- The Qur'an says we are to feed the hungry because we love Allah, without wanting any reward or any thanks. Do you think it is easy to do good things because we love God and God asks us to do them, without expecting any special reward? Do you ever do good things so that your parents or friends will reward you?
- If you do good things at home or at school without expecting a reward, are you ever pleased to find that you do receive some special attention? Do you think God will reward good even when we have not expected it?

Both Muslims and Christians teach that God wants those who are able to give to poor, hungry, and needy people (as well as give to take care of mosques, churches, religious organizations, and the people who take care of them). Muslims talk about *zakat*—called "giving alms" in English words we don't use very often. Christians talk about giving "tithes and offerings"—also words that are not often used outside a church. Both *zakat* and the tithe are based on the idea of giving a certain percentage of what we have earned or what we have. Christians say they are giving back to God a part of what God has given to them: God is the Creator who has made everything for our use; God controls the world and its people; and God loves us. *Zakat* is also given as a thanksgiving to God, something we owe to God for what he has trusted us to have and use. *Sadaga* is a voluntary giving, whenever a person wants to help someone else. It does not have to be financial help. The Qur'an says that even a smile is *sadaga* (charity).

Both *zakat* and tithes are based on what is called "proportionate" giving, in which a specific percentage is given. The systems for figuring the amount and for giving are different. In particular, Muslim calculations are based on total assets every year, while Christian calculations (tithes), though a higher percentage, are figured on annual income only. Another difference is that while the Christian tithe is only recommended, the Muslim *zakat* is required for everyone who lives above poverty level.

- ❷ What kinds of people in *our* city/town/county are especially in need of help? (Are they hungry? Homeless? Without jobs? Sick? Paying too much money for medical expenses?) Who are working to help these people? Are there ways that we can help? Are there things we can do even if we don't have money to give?
- ❷ Are there people that need help who live farther away from us? What kinds of needs do they have? Who is helping them? Can we do anything to help?
- ❷ You may wish to talk about the Islamic emphasis on justice. God's guidance teaches us to live justly. What is justice? How is helping those in need related to justice?

Activities
- Work on a project together to meet some kind of local community need or some known national need that is not tied to any one religious community. For example, make kits to be used for hurricane relief the next time there is a major disaster. (Find an organization that stores these kits in advance. Ask what they want in each kit and bring the necessary equipment so that the children can do the preparation during this session.)
- If you have a Christian-Muslim group of children and if adults of the two communities are ready to assist them on a continuing basis, talk about ways the children might do more together that would help other people— either on some regular basis or at an appropriate future time when need arises. Approach adults in advance to check on possibilities, based on the concept that Muslims and Christians live together and should seek the common good of one another and of others together.

Closing

At the end of your time, gather together to say thank you for this time of learning over the eight sessions. If your group is made up of all Christian children and you have made a list of things you have learned about Islam, use the list to talk about how your knowledge of Islam and Muslims will affect your thinking and behavior. Talk about the Muslim as the neighbor in Jesus' commandment to love the neighbor as the self.

In closing, name some things for which you want to thank God. Plan some simple way of expressing thanks for these things.

Activities Instruction Section

The instructions include some directions for photocopying that will not be necessary if every child has a book from which to see the visual instructions and examples directly. Urge children with books to bring them to each session.

Unit 1 The First Stories

A. Form the Word "Allah" from Chenille Stems
For this activity, you will need:
- Chenille stems, preferably green (one per child)
- Photocopies of "Information about Muslim Writing" (see pages 237–238)

Pass out copies of "Information about Muslim Writing" and read through the pages with the children. Have the children shape the word "Allah" in stylized form using a chenille stem. Have them look at the different ways the word "Allah" is written on the page, or follow the example of the photograph of a chenille stem below. Remind the children that Arabic can be written in very simple forms, so they can use their imaginations. Invite the children to share their creations.

Activities Instruction Section

B. Make a Lamp

For this activity, you will need:
- ❏ Sheet of paper (8 1/2" x 11" works fine, but any rectangular sheet of plain or decorative paper is appropriate)
- ❏ Scissors
- ❏ Tea light (or votive) candles
- ❏ Pencils

One type of lamp hung in mosques is made of metal that has cut-out parts through which the light shines. In this activity the children will make paper lamps, with cutouts, that sit on a table.

CAUTION: Never leave a lit candle unattended!

Directions:
1. Take a rectangular sheet of paper and divide its length into four even parts by folding.

2. Unfold the paper and fold it in half lengthwise.

3. Fold the center of the paper up, as shown, and cut along the lengthwise fold. This will leave an opening in the middle of the sheet of paper.

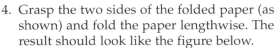

4. Grasp the two sides of the folded paper (as shown) and fold the paper lengthwise. The result should look like the figure below.

5. Keeping the paper folds together, draw and cut a pattern that will be on opposite sides of the lamp. At home, place a small tea light candle inside and enjoy!

226

C. Listen to the Call to Prayer

For this activity, you will need:
- ❏ A recording of the call to prayer
- ❏ Tape or CD player

Unless you have a recording, you may want to search—or have someone else search—on the Web for an audio of the *adhan*. It can be found at www.islamonline.net/english/introducingislam/Worship/Prayers/article03.shtml (on the right of the Web page, click on Listen to the *adhan*).

D. Write the *Bismillah*

For this activity, you will need:
- ❏ Paper
- ❏ Felt-tip markers, crayons, or other writing instruments

On a piece of paper, have the children write "In the name of God, the Merciful, the Compassionate" or "In the name of God" in English. Have them look at the description about Arabic and the writing of the word "Allah" for ideas about different ways of writing that are used in Arabic (see page 225). Some of the children may be inspired to explore different ways of writing in English. The words should be written in a dignified style, though they may be playfully creative.

Activities Instruction Section

Unit 2 Ibrahim/Abraham

A. Make a Ka'ba Cube

For this activity, you will need:
- Paper plates
- Small box, roughly square in shape
- Black felt-tip markers (preferably with a large tip and strong black color)
- Black construction paper (*optional*)
- Glue (*optional*)
- Paper (*optional*)
- Photocopies of "Cube Pattern" on page 239 (*optional*)
- Tape (*optional*)

The Ka'ba is a cube-shaped building in the courtyard of the Grand Mosque in Mecca. It is the center of the *hajj* activities. For this project, we will create a small model of the Ka'ba. Although the Ka'ba is symbolically a cube, the actual building is not exact in its measurements, so don't worry if the materials you are using are only roughly cubic in shape.

Directions:
1. In the center of the paper plate, have the children mark a black dot. This will represent the symbolic center of Mecca.
2. Pass out small boxes. The box will represent the Ka'ba. If you cannot find a small box, the children can use the "Cube Pattern" on page 239 to make a cube.
3. Every year before the pilgrimage month, a new black cloth is made to cover the Ka'ba. Have them color their boxes black with a marker. If you want to make the project even more realistic, you can have them cut a sheet of black paper and glue it to the top of the box and fold the sides down to represent the black cloth covering the Ka'ba.
4. Place glue in the center of the plate and glue the box down, covering the black dot that the children drew in step 1.
5. The Ka'ba now sits in the center of the circle of the plate. This represents the circular path that pilgrims travel, going round and round the Ka'ba during the *hajj*. During prayer times, pilgrims surround the Ka'ba in a circular row, facing the Ka'ba to stand, kneel, and prostrate themselves in prayer.

Study Guide

B. Learn about Mathematical Symbolism and the Ka'ba
For this advanced individual activity for interested older children, you will need:
❏ Photocopies of page "Math in Muslim Thought" (page 240)

One or more children, a parent, or a teacher may be interested in reading the explanation of the mathematical symbolism in the Ka'ba in "Math in Muslim Thought" and making a simple report about it to a larger group of children.

C. Look at Pictures of the Ka'ba
If you want further pictures of the *hajj* and the Ka'ba, go to www.photoarchive.Saudiaramcoworld.com/ on the Web and use its search engine to look for pictures. Alternately, purchase the DVD "Inside Mecca," distributed by *National Geographic* and produced by an American Muslim journalist, Anisa Mehdi, in 2003 (available for online purchase from Amazon). (Note that the imagery of Muhammad and his family in the DVD is objectionable to some Muslims who adhere to the Muslim tradition of not picturing Muhammad.)

Activities Instruction Section

Unit 3 Ya'kub/Jacob

Make a Plaque Activities
For the activities, you will need:
- Paper plates (use a heavy quality if you are able)
- Writing instruments if the children will be writing in the middle of the plate—for activities A and B
- Photocopies of "The Ninety-nine Names of God" (page 244)—for activity B
- Photocopies of "The *Bismillah*" (page 243) on heavy paper or light cardboard—for activity C
- Glue—for activity C
- Scissors—for activity C

A. Write *Inshallah*
Write the words "God willing" or "inshallah" in the middle of the plate. Make sure the children leave room for a border (to be made in the next session) but fill the remaining space with the word or words.

B. Write One of the Names of God
Have the children pick a name from the list on page 244, then write it in the middle of the plate, again leaving room for a border but filling the remaining space from the sides of the plate.

C. Paste the *Bismillah* on the plaque
Cut out the *Bismillah* on the reproducible page, and then glue the words onto the plate. The paper plate will dry best if a weight is placed over it.

Study Guide

Units 4 and 5 Musa/Moses and the Desert Journey

A. Make a Border for the Plaque (started during the previous session)
For this activity, you will need:
❏ Pencils
❏ Crayons, colored pencils, watercolors and a brush, or markers

Muslims often use designs made from geometric shapes and from things seen in nature. These are often made into intricate interwoven patterns. In this project, you will create a design to put around the edges of the plaque you started during your last session. Use the designs you see here to give you ideas about making a border. Make the outlines of the border then color in the design. When you have finished, you can fasten the plaque on a wall or give it as a gift.

This is an example of calligraphy inside a border design.

231

Activities Instruction Section

B. Color Geometric Islamic Patterns

For this activity, you will need:
- Photocopies of "Geometric Patterns" (pages 245–247)
- Crayons, colored pencils, watercolors and a brush, or markers
- Scissors
- Tape or glue (*optional*)
- Large sheets of paper or light cardboard (*optional*)

Pass out copies of "Geometric Patterns" (see pages 245–247). Have the children use crayons, colored pencils, watercolors and a brush, or markers to color in the patterns. Look first to see what the design in the pattern is, then take time to decide how to color it before you begin. Select only three to five colors and fill in the whole design. Here are some ideas for possible ways to color in the patterns:

1. Fill in the patterns so that all the colors interact harmoniously with one another, or fill in the patterns so that there is a lot of contrast and excitement between the colors.
2. Color the pattern so that areas are left white—either the background or the main part of the design.

If you wish, make a large display of your pattern. Color several pages of the same square pattern, using the same colors for each one. On each sheet of paper, cut the design at its edges so that it will fit the pattern on another piece of paper together. Fasten the sheets together with tape or mount them with glue on a larger sheet of paper or cardboard. See the way the designs can be made to keep going on and on, to fit whatever amount of space you wish!

> If this project particularly appeals to the children, more patterns are available in a paperback book by J. Bourgoin, *Arabic Geometrical Pattern & Design* (New York: Dover Publications, 1973), available from an online bookseller. Additionally, a Web site with computer-generated Islamic star patterns is www.members.tripod.com/vismath4/kaplan. Please note that, though it says that the traditional methods for creating these patterns are "lost to history," this is incorrect.

Unit 6 Guides, Judges, and Kings

A. Make a Reed Pen

For this activity, you will need:
- 6–8 inch length of stiff reed or a thin stalk of bamboo for each child
- 1 or 2 sharp craft knives
- Fine sandpaper (one sheet for each child)

Muslims talk about the miracle of Muhammad receiving the Qur'an and its being written down as dictated to Muhammad by the angel Jabra'il. The pen (*qalam*) is important as the tool by which the sacred words were written down. The traditional *qalam* is cut from a stiff hollow reed, and it is still used for writing beautiful Arabic calligraphy. In many countries, schoolchildren learn to write with such a pen and are taught how to cut their own pens. Often schoolchildren have a sample of what they are to write at the top of the page on which they will be writing.

> **CAUTION:** This activity should be done only by those who can handle a sharp knife safely and who can follow the instruction to always cut with the knife motion pointing away from the hands and body. It is recommended that a special "cutting station" be set up where one person at a time can do this activity with adult supervision.
>
> If it is decided not to do knife cutting during the session, the teacher/parent may cut several pens in advance and make them available for children to use during the session.

Step 1. Select a length of stiff reed or a thin stalk of bamboo. Trim one end of the piece of reed or bamboo so it is completely free from cracks or frayed edges.

Step 2. At the trimmed end of the reed or bamboo, cut away a pen tip using a sharp craft knife. The cut should begin about three-quarters of an inch from the end and curve gently down to the end of the reed.

Step 3. After cutting the curve in the reed, use the knife to make a straight cut across the tip. The reed should be quite thin at the place where you make this cut. The thickness of the letters you write will be determined by how wide a tip you make on your pen. After cutting, use a piece of very fine sandpaper gently to smooth the tip of your pen.

Step 4. Using the tip of the craft knife, gently make a shallow cut down the centerline of the inside of the pen tip. Make a shallow cut only; do not cut all the way through the reed. This cut will help guide ink to the tip of the pen.

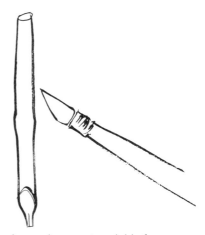

Your pen is complete. You may go on to the activity of writing with your new *qalam*.

B. Write Arabic

For this activity, you will need:
- Paper
- The reed or bamboo pen made earlier or a calligraphy marker pen (available from most office or art supply stores)
- Bottles of India ink for the reed or bamboo pen
- Photocopies of "The *Bismillah*" (see page 243)

In this activity, you will write the beginning words of the *Bismillah* in Arabic, ("*bism Allah*," meaning "in the name of God"). Nearly every project of a Muslim is begun with these words of prayer, so it is fitting that this will be your first use of a reed pen, if that is what you will be using. Those who do not have reed pens can do this project with another pen.

To write, hold your pen so that the tip is almost vertical in relation to the line of writing. Dip the reed pen in the ink, wipe off any excess ink on a piece of scrap paper, and then begin forming the letters. Dip your reed pen each time that the ink runs low. After practicing the basics of using your pen, write the words "bism Allah" in Arabic. Remember to write starting from the right side of the paper and moving left.

TIP: One trick schoolchildren use is to place a ball of cotton in the ink bottle. This makes it easier to get the right amount of ink on your pen tip.

If your pen is held correctly, vertical lines should be narrower and horizontal lines should be thicker. Two examples of the *Bismillah* words are shown.

An alternative to using the reed or bamboo pen is to use a thick felt tip pen with a broad, flat nib to do your writing. These are sold as calligraphy markers in most office supply or art stores.

Study Guide

Unit 7 The Births of Jesus/'Isa and John/Yahya

Prepare Food to Eat Together
For this activity, you will need:
- ❏ Foods for the recipes you plan to use (see below)
- ❏ Appropriate kitchen utensils
- ❏ Large tablecloth
- ❏ Serving dishes, paper plates and cups, tableware, as needed

Prepare food that can be eaten together. While Middle Eastern food is suggested, you may find that someone has simple recipes from some other part of the world in which Muslims live. If you have Muslims in your group or have invited one or more Muslims to help with food preparation, you can be guided by what they are able to make with the children and by what they indicate is appropriate.

You may focus your attention on the food preparation, ending with an eating time; or, you may decide to have a minimal amount of food and spend your time organizing a spot for eating and enjoying one or two very simple foods together.

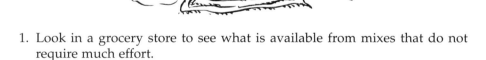

1. Look in a grocery store to see what is available from mixes that do not require much effort.

- Look for hummus (either canned or in a package of the dry ingredients to which water is added). This can be used as a dip to be eaten with pita bread. Allow the children to help prepare the hummus and to cut or tear the pita bread into smaller pieces.
- Look for couscous that can be mixed with water. If you wish to add ingredients, use dried apricots cut into pieces with kitchen scissors, broken walnut or pecan pieces, and/or raisins. Plump the apricots and raisins in warm water before adding.
- Check to see if there is a tabbouleh mix that only requires minimal work—perhaps the adding of tomatoes.

CAUTION: You may be using boiling water. If so, pour the water away from the place where the children are gathered, then allow the children to stir what you have put into the bowl.

2. Use simple recipes to prepare foods, timing your food preparation so that they will be ready when you need them. Here are a couple of possible recipes. You may find others.

Sekanjebin (a refreshing drink)
1 pound sugar
6 sprigs fresh mint
1/2 cup white vinegar
1 cup water (or sufficient amount to cover the sugar)

Bring the sugar and water to a boil and skim off any foam that has collected. Add mint and vinegar and boil until the syrup has slightly thickened. Remove the mint sprigs and pour the syrup into a container to cool.
When ready to serve, put two tablespoons of the syrup in the bottom of a glass and fill with water and ice. Stir well.

Pistachio Ice Cream
Ice cream
Pistachios
Rose water

Soften the ice cream just sufficiently to be able to mix additional ingredients into it. In the meantime, break up pistachio nuts into smaller pieces. Place the softened ice cream into a bowl and stir in the broken nuts and a few drops of rose water. Sample the ice cream and cautiously add more rose water until it tastes like you want it. Place the ice cream in a container and return it to the freezer until it has hardened sufficiently to eat.

Reproducible Resources

Unit 1 The First Stories

Information about Muslim Writing

The Qur'an is the sacred book of Muslims. They believe that the words of the Qur'an are God's own words. Because of this, Muslims use beautiful writing of words as a form of art. The art of beautiful writing is called "calligraphy" in English.

In the Muslim use of calligraphy, the same thing can be written in many styles, and it can be created out of many different materials: woven into cloth, made out of bricks, carved in wood or plaster, or written with pen and ink.

In this project, we will learn a little about the Arabic script in which the Qur'an is written, and we will learn to recognize the word "Allah" when it is written in different forms.

The Arabic script is similar to the Latin script used to write English in several ways:

- A script is a way of writing a language, but it is not the same thing as a language.
- Both the Arabic and the Latin scripts are used to write many different languages. For example, the Latin script is used to write English, Spanish, French, German, and Turkish. The Arabic script is used to write Arabic, Persian, Kurdish, Urdu, Dari, Baluchi, Sindhi, and other languages.
- Both Latin and Arabic are phonetic writing systems. This means that their letters stand for individual sounds.

The Arabic script is different from the Latin script in several ways:

- The Arabic script is written from right to left. The Latin script is written from left to right.
- Many of the letters of the Arabic script are always attached to one another.
- Some of the vowel sounds are not always written down.

Here is the word "Allah" written in very different styles. Can you see the word "Allah" in each example? Can you find the word "Allah" written in the geometric pattern at the right below?

We will use a very unusual material to write the word "Allah"—chenille stems, often called pipe cleaners! It is particularly appropriate to do this project in green, the color most beloved in Islam. Remember, the Muslim religion began in the desert, and in the desert, green is the color of life!

Unit 2 Ibrahim/Abraham

Ka'ba Cube Pattern

Directions: Photocopy the pattern onto card stock or heavy paper. Make one copy for each child. Have the children cut out the cube pattern and fold it along the lines to form into a cube. Have them tuck the tab edges inside the cube and tape them close.

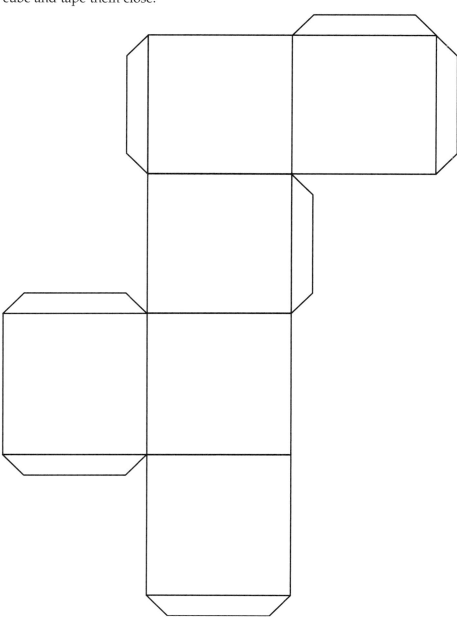

B. Math in Muslim Thought

The diagram below shows the interplay of symbolism, mathematics, and design in Islamic thought. Beginning from a single point at the center of this diagram, three lines move outward to create the points needed to draw a six-sided shape that can also be viewed as representing a three-dimensional cube.

Returning to the flat surface drawing, a triangle can be drawn connecting three of the edges of the cube. From this relationship a series of lines parallel to sides of the cube are drawn so as to form a three-dimensional ball, with sides in the form of triangles, such that the edges of the ball touch the planar surfaces of the cube.

Working back and forth from two-dimensional to three-dimensional viewpoints is the basis for many complex Islamic patterns, as well as for the proportions of buildings, the engineering of vaults and domes, and the development of the disciplines of algebra, geometry, and astronomy.

- On a symbolic level, the point can be seen as the simplest geometric reality, representing the meteor housed in the wall of the Ka'ba, symbolic of the center, the one, the underlying eternal unity of the creator.
- Two points create a line, the first extension of divine unity into physical creation, representing the intellect.
- Three points create the simplest enclosed space, the triangle, representing the soul.
- Four points create a square—and by extension a cube—representing matter.

The cube of the Ka'ba can now be more fully understood as the relationship between the creator, the intellect, the soul, and physical reality, all surrounded by the concentric circles of pilgrims and by all the further concentric circles of Muslims praying as they face the Ka'ba from all over the world.

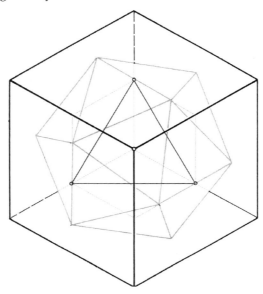

C. Postage Stamps 1

Reproducible Resources

C. Postage Stamps 2

Unit 3 Ya'kub/Jacob

A. The *Bismillah*

Note: You will need to enlarge the picture until the circle is seven inches in diameter. Make a copy for each child.

Reproducible Resources

B. The Ninety-nine Names of God

In the name of Allah, the Compassionate, the Merciful.
Allah is God; there is no god but Allah.

ALLAH

- The Beneficent
- The Merciful
- The Sovereign Lord
- The Holy
- The Source of Peace
- The Guardian of Faith
- The Protector
- The Mighty
- The Compeller
- The Majestic
- The Creator
- The Evolver
- The Fashioner
- The Forgiver
- The Subduer
- The Bestower
- The Provider
- The Opener
- The All-Knowing
- The Constrictor
- The Expender
- The Abaser
- The Exalter
- The Honorer
- The Dishonorer
- The All-Hearing
- The All-Seeing
- The Judge
- The Just
- The Subtle One
- The Aware
- The Forbearing One
- The Great One
- The All-Forgiving
- The Appreciative
- The Most High
- The Most Great
- The Preserver
- The Maintainer
- *The Reckoner
- The Sublime One
- The Generous One
- The Watchful
- The Responsive
- The All-Embracing
- The Wise
- The Loving
- The Most Glorious One
- The Resurrector
- The Witness
- The Truth
- The Trustee
- The Most Strong
- The Firm One
- The Protecting Friend
- The Praiseworthy
- *The Reckoner
- The Originator
- The Restorer
- The Giver of Life
- The Creator of Death
- The Alive
- The Self-subsisting
- The Finder
- The Noble
- The Unique
- The One
- The Eternal
- The Able
- The Powerful
- The Expediter
- The Delayer
- The First
- The Last
- The Manifest
- The Hidden
- The Governor
- The Most Exalted
- The Source of All Goodness
- The Acceptor of Repentance
- The Avenger
- The Pardoner
- The Compassionate
- The Eternal Owner of Sovereignty
- The Lord of Majesty and Bounty
- The Equitable
- The Gatherer
- The Self-Sufficient
- The Enricher
- The Preventer
- The Distresser
- The Propitious
- The Light
- The Guide
- The Incomparable
- The Everlasting
- The Supreme Inheritor
- The Guide to the Right Path
- The Patient

*different Arabic words used

A list of the Ninety-nine Names in Arabic and English is available on the Web at www.noorulislambolton.com/names_allah.asp.

Study Guide

Units 4 and 5 Musa/Moses and The Desert Journey

Geometric Patterns

Geometric Patterns

Geometric Patterns

Unit 6 Guides, Judges, and Kings

Psalm 103

¹ **With all my heart**
  I praise the Lord,
and with all that I am
  I praise his holy name!
² **With all my heart**
  I praise the Lord!
I will never forget
  how kind he has been.
³ **The Lord forgives our sins,**
heals us when we are sick,
⁴ and protects us from death.
His kindness and love
  are a crown on our heads.
⁵ Each day that we live,
  he provides for our needs
and gives us the strength
  of a young eagle.
⁶ For all who are mistreated,
  the Lord brings justice.
⁷ He taught his Law to Moses
and showed all Israel
  what he could do.
⁸ **The Lord is merciful!**
He is kind and patient,
  and his love never fails.
⁹ The Lord won't always be angry
  and point out our sins;
¹⁰ he doesn't punish us
  as our sins deserve.
¹¹ How great is God's love for all
  who worship him?
Greater than the distance
  between heaven and earth!
¹² How far has the Lord taken
  our sins from us?
Farther than the distance
  from east to west!
¹³ Just as parents are kind
  to their children,
the Lord is kind
  to all who worship him,
¹⁴ because he knows
  we are made of dust.
¹⁵ We humans are like grass
or wild flowers
  that quickly bloom.
¹⁶ But a scorching wind blows,
and they quickly wither
  to be forever forgotten.
¹⁷ **The Lord is always kind**
  to those who worship him,
and he keeps his promises
to their descendants
  ¹⁸ who faithfully obey him.
¹⁹ God has set up his kingdom
in heaven, and he rules
  the whole creation.
²⁰ All of you mighty angels,
who obey God's commands,
  come and praise your Lord!
²¹ All of you thousands
who serve and obey God,
  come and praise your Lord!
²² All of God's creation
and all that he rules,
  come and praise your Lord!
With all my heart
  I praise the Lord!

—Contemporary English Version

Glossary

adhan	the call to prayer
bani adam	offspring of Adam ("everyone")
Bismillah	"In the name of God, the Merciful, the Compassionate"
dua	a form of supplication and praise that is freer than *salat*
hadith	the traditional reports of Muhammad's deeds and sayings
hajj	the annual pilgrimage that Muslim faithful make to Mecca
hijra	the migration to Medina in the year 622 C.E.
'Id al-Adha	the Feast of Sacrifice
iftar	a meal at the time a fast is completed for the day
Injil	the Gospel
inshallah	"God willing"
Ka'ba	the ancient shrine on the spot where Muslims believe that Abraham built the first House of God
Kalim Allah	"the word of God"
khalifa	a godly prophet-king who is the representative of God to judge with justice
Masih	Messiah
mihrab	the niche in a mosque, showing the direction to face for prayer
minbar	a pulpit
nabi	a prophet
qalam	a pen cut from a stiff hollow reed
rasul	a messenger
sadaq	charity
salat	rituals of prayer; the prescribed ritual prayers
sawm	fasting
shahada	the witness and confession of Muslims: "I witness that there is no god except God and that Muhammad is God's prophet."
shari'ah	Islamic law, which is based on the Qur'an
shirk	idolatry; the association of anything with God
tasbih	a string of beads Muslims use to recite the Ninety-nine Names of God

Glossary

tawaf	a ritual in which Muslim pilgrims walk around the Ka'ba three times during the *hajj*
Tawrat	the Torah
umma	the one community of all the people of Islam
wudu	ritual washing, which precedes the prayers
Zabur	the Psalms
zakat	alms giving; giving for the poor and needy